PREFACE

1. Scope

This publication provides joint doctrine and information for the planning, preparation, and execution of legal support to joint military operations.

2. Purpose

This publication has been prepared under the direction of the Chairman of the Joint Chiefs of Staff, and has been reviewed favorably by the General Counsel of the Department of Defense as the Chief Legal Officer of the Department. It sets forth joint doctrine to guide the activities and performance of the Armed Forces of the United States in operations and provides the doctrinal basis for interagency coordination and for US military involvement in multinational operations. It provides military guidance for the exercise of authority by combatant commanders and other joint force commanders (JFCs) and prescribes joint doctrine for operations and training. It provides military guidance for use by the Armed Forces in preparing their appropriate plans. This publication is not intended to restrict the authority of the JFC in organizing the force and executing the mission in a manner the JFC deems most appropriate to ensure unity of effort in the accomplishment of the overall objective.

3. Application

a. Joint doctrine established in this publication applies to the commanders of combatant commands, subunified commands, joint task forces, subordinate components of these commands, and the Services.

b. The guidance in this publication is authoritative; as such, this doctrine will be followed except when, in the judgment of the commander, exceptional circumstances dictate otherwise. If conflicts arise between the contents of this publication and the contents of Service publications, this publication will take precedence unless the Chairman of the Joint Chiefs of Staff, normally in coordination with the other members of the Joint Chiefs of Staff, has provided more current and specific guidance. Commanders of forces operating as part of a multinational (alliance or coalition) military command should follow multinational doctrine and procedures approved by the United States. For doctrine and procedures not approved by the United States, commanders should evaluate and follow the multinational command's doctrine and procedures, where applicable and consistent with US law, regulations, and doctrine.

For the Chairman of the Joint Chiefs of Staff:

William E. Gortney
VADM, USN
Director, Joint Staff

SUMMARY OF CHANGES
REVISION OF JOINT PUBLICATION 1-04
DATED 01 MARCH 2007

- **Deleted Department of Defense combat support agency legal counsel descriptions**

- **Added the law of war principles of military necessity, unnecessary suffering, distinction, and proportionality**

- **Added a description of duties for the Chief Counsel, National Guard Bureau**

- **Inserted language that includes staff judge advocate advice on funding of military operations and the obligation and expenditure of appropriated funds**

- **Inserted language that describes domestic operations requirements**

- **Inserted language on cyberspace**

- **Updated the reference to the foreign clearance guide**

Intentionally Blank

TABLE OF CONTENTS

GLOSSARY

FIGURE

- **Presents Legal Organizations, Missions, and Functions**

- **Describes Legal Support to Joint Operations Planning**

- **Discusses Legal Support to the Joint Task Force**

Legal Organizations, Missions, and Functions

To ensure unity of effort, both the joint force commander and the joint force staff judge advocate (SJA) must have a common understanding of who is responsible for performing which legal tasks at each level of military operations and how those tasks are performed.

Legal organizations within the Department of Defense (DOD) that support joint operations perform a wide variety of tasks at the strategic, operational, and tactical levels. Although each legal organization may possess similar functional capabilities (e.g., international and operational law advice, fiscal and contract law reviews, the provision of claims, criminal law, and legal assistance services), the specific tasks performed within each of those functional capabilities differ in purpose and scope depending on the level of military operations and the organization performing them.

General Counsel of the Department of Defense.

The DOD General Counsel (GC) provides legal advice to the Secretary and Deputy Secretary of Defense on all legal matters and services performed within, or involving, DOD. The DOD GC coordinates and promotes cooperation and mutual understanding among DOD components and between DOD and other government agencies on issues ranging from mergers and acquisitions involving defense suppliers, to significant litigation in which the Department of Justice represents DOD interests.

General Counsel of Combat Support Agencies.

There are 15 DOD agencies and seven DOD field activities that operate under the authority, direction, and control of the Secretary of Defense (SecDef). These organizations provide support and services in specified functional areas to the combatant commands and the rest of DOD.

Legal Counsel, Office of the Chairman of the Joint Chiefs of Staff.

The Legal Counsel (LC) advises the Chairman of the Joint Chiefs of Staff (CJCS), Vice CJCS, joint directors, and Joint Staff on the full spectrum of legal issues. Given the CJCS role as spokesman for the combatant commanders

(CCDRs), the LC frequently advises and assists the CCDRs' legal staffs. As directed by CJCS, the LC represents the CJCS in the US interagency process, and in coordination with the respective geographic CCDR's staff judge advocate (SJA), in discussions and negotiations with foreign governments and nongovernmental organizations.

Joint Force SJA.

The joint force SJA (also titled "the judge advocate" or "command judge advocate") is the principal legal advisor to the joint force commander (JFC) and a key member of a JFC's personal staff. The joint force SJA is the principal legal advisor to the CCDR, deputy commander, and chief of staff; and they coordinate as necessary with the legal staff of the other combatant commands. A combatant command SJA coordinates, as necessary, with the legal staffs at the Office of the Secretary of Defense, Joint Chiefs of Staff, and the Military Departments. The joint force SJA reports directly to the JFC. In the contemporary operating environment, the joint force SJA provides the full spectrum of legal support through direct and reachback capability to joint operations across the range of military operations.

Legal Support to Joint Operations Planning

Legal advisors support their organizations in carrying out their planning responsibilities by providing legal advice on the myriad of regulations, laws, policies, treaties, and agreements that apply to joint military operations.

Legal advisors actively participate in the entire planning process from joint intelligence preparation of the operational environment development, to mission analysis, to course of action development and recommendation, through execution. Strategic and operational planning typically occurs at the joint task force (JTF) and higher echelons. Legal advisors who perform planning tasks at the tactical level typically do so as a Service component of a JTF.

Law of War Principles.

It is DOD policy that members of the DOD components comply with the law of war during all armed conflicts, however such conflicts are characterized, and in all other military operations. Some of the law of war principles to be considered during the planning process are as follows:

Military Necessity. The principle of military necessity justifies those measures not forbidden by international law that are indispensable for securing the complete submission of the enemy as soon as possible.

Unnecessary Suffering. The principle of unnecessary suffering forbids the employment of means and methods of warfare calculated to cause unnecessary suffering. This principle acknowledges that combatants' necessary suffering, which may include severe injury and loss of life, is lawful. This principle largely applies to the legality of weapons and ammunition.

Distinction. This principle requires parties to a conflict to distinguish between combatants and noncombatants and to distinguish between military objectives and protected property and places. Parties to a conflict must direct their operations only against military objectives.

Proportionality. The principle of proportionality prohibits attacks that may be expected to cause incidental loss of civilian life, injury to civilians, damage to civilian objects, or a combination thereof, which would be excessive in relation to the concrete and direct military advantage expected to be gained. As such, this principle is only applicable when an attack may possibly affect civilians or civilian objects, and thereby, may cause collateral damage.

Legal Support to Strategic Level Planning.

The strategic-level planning processes within the National Security Council System; Planning, Programming, Budgeting, and Execution process; the Joint Strategic Planning System; and the Adaptive Planning and Execution system take place primarily between the President and/or SecDef, the CJCS, and the CCDRs. Their legal advisors—the DOD GC, the LC, and the CCDRs' SJAs—plan and coordinate DOD-wide and theater-level legal support for the full range of planning activities including mobilization, deployment, employment, sustainment, redeployment, and demobilization of forces.

Legal Support to Operational Level Planning.

At the operational level, the supported CCDR may retain planning responsibility or delegate planning responsibility to a subordinate JFC, typically the commander of a JTF or a Service component commander. Regardless of the level of command, the legal advisor has a key support role in developing legally sufficient plans and orders that support achievement of the operational objectives. During the joint operation planning process, the joint force SJA prepares the legal estimate, plans legal support for the joint force, and contributes to the overall planning effort.

Legal Support to the Joint Task Force

As the principal legal advisor to the commander, joint task force (CJTF) and JTF staff, the JTF SJA is responsible for the organization and employment of legal personnel assigned or attached to the JTF headquarters (HQ). The JTF SJA provides full spectrum legal service to the JTF HQ and coordinates with the supported CCDR's SJA and supporting component SJAs to optimize legal support throughout the JTF.

Legal Support in the Joint Task Force (JTF) Battle Rhythm.

Each JTF develops a battle rhythm of daily events, briefings, and meetings that optimizes the information flow across the staff, allowing the organization to plan and execute the mission most effectively. An effective JTF SJA understands the JTF battle rhythm, as well as the collaborative information environment, and actively provides legal advice and counsel to the boards, centers, cells, and working groups of the JTF.

Forming the JTF SJA Section.

Joint force SJAs at all levels are responsible for developing the organizational structure for their command SJA sections; but, unlike the JTF SJA, most are not required to form at the same time they are planning, training, and deploying for an operation. Because JTFs are established in a variety of different ways and for diverse missions, it is critically important for a JTF SJA to understand fully the legal support requirements of the particular JTF and how those requirements may change over time.

JTF SJA Manning.

Designation as a JTF SJA often requires a transition from a single Service perspective to a broader joint operational view.

SecDef and CCDRs have many options in establishing a JTF HQ. The JTF HQ can be established either by using a standing JTF HQ, by augmenting a core Service component HQ, or by forming an ad hoc HQ from multiple services. The JTF SJA develops the personnel requirements for the SJA section and submits them to the manpower and personnel directorate for inclusion in the CJTF's proposed joint manning document. Although there is variability in staffing requirements for each JTF due to the factors listed above, a typical land-based JTF must be capable of operating on a 24-hour battle rhythm.

Joint SJA Training.

There are two components of joint SJA training—individual and organizational.

Individual Joint Training. To ensure that the JTF SJA section can provide adequate legal support to the JTF, the

SJA must ensure that assigned or attached personnel have the requisite individual training. All members of the JTF SJA section must have training in three areas—legal, joint, and tactical.

Organizational JTF SJA Training. The JTF SJAs organizational training responsibilities fall into two categories, SJA section training and CJTF and staff training.

SJA Section Training. Successful legal support to the JTF depends on a well-integrated legal team where each member of the section understands the overall JTF mission, the operations of the JTF, the responsibilities of the JTF SJA section, and their specific role within the organization.

JTF Command and Staff Training. The SJA typically provides training on the following: law of armed conflict; rules of engagement/rules for the use of force; host country or applicable domestic law; detention operations; ethics and standards of conduct; procurement/fiscal considerations and constraints; claims process; and other legal issues identified in the mission analysis.

Equipping the JTF SJA.

Although Service component SJA offices often have organic equipment to perform their Service-specific legal support, a JTF SJA section typically will not have the organic equipment that is necessary to perform the entire joint legal support mission. The same factors that drive the manning requirements will affect the JTF SJA determination of the section's equipment and logistics requirements. The mission, environment, composition of the joint force, size of the SJA section, JTF battle rhythm, and location of the section personnel supporting the boards, centers, and cells, are key factors affecting the equipment requirements.

Deployment.

Deployment marks the beginning of the execution phase of the operation. Prior to a main body deployment, the JTF SJA researches and determines what legal authorities are in place and what legal authorities are necessary or desired to support the JTF mission. Authorities regarding the status, overflight, and ground transit of forces are usually most critical at this stage. The CJTF and higher HQ must be alerted to any legal deficiencies as soon as possible to allow them to coordinate and address the deficiency.

Employment.

A member of the JFC's personal staff, the JTF SJA is an essential advisor on the myriad of legal issues associated with combat and noncombat operations. The JTF SJA ensures that the CJTF understands the laws, policies, treaties, and agreements that apply to US relations with the governments and inhabitants of foreign nations in the JTF's joint operations area and how those laws, policies, treaties, and agreements may affect current and future JTF operations. The JTF SJA assists the CJTF in monitoring, assessing, planning, coordinating, directing, and controlling operations through direct participation on JTF boards, centers, cells, and working groups.

Transition.

The JTF SJA is responsible for transitioning legal support responsibilities to follow-on forces. Transition may occur between the JTF and another US command, a foreign command (e.g., host nation or United Nations forces), or an organization under civilian control. Both organizations must prepare for and coordinate the transition to ensure an orderly transfer of authority and responsibility.

Redeployment.

Redeployment may begin at any point during JTF operations, so redeployment planning should begin as soon as possible. During redeployment, the JTF SJA sets section movement priorities; provides priorities and guidance for section recovery and reconstitution; and determines if deployment of additional personnel is required to assist with section redeployment activities.

Lessons Learned.

During execution, transition, and redeployment, the JTF SJA and legal section should capture and chronicle legal lessons learned. Use of lessons learned will ensure succeeding SJAs will have the benefit of the experiences of their predecessors. Lessons learned should include, among other concerns, legal issues and access to resources including reach-back support to resolve them, equipment, billeting, personnel legal specialties, non-lawyer skill requirements, tour length appropriateness, and other operational matters that affect the provision of legal services.

CONCLUSION

This publication provides joint doctrine and information for the planning, preparation, and execution of legal support to joint military operations.

CHAPTER I
LEGAL ORGANIZATIONS, MISSIONS, AND FUNCTIONS

> *"It is also clear from the commanders who testified that legal advice is essential to effective combat operations in the current environment—legal advice is now part of the tooth not the tail."*
>
> **Section 574, 2005 National Defense Authorization Act, Independent Review Panel to Study the Relationship between Military Department General Counsels and Judge Advocates General**
> **15 September 2005**

1. Introduction

Legal organizations within the Department of Defense (DOD) that support joint operations perform a wide variety of tasks at the strategic, operational, and tactical levels. Although each legal organization may possess similar functional capabilities (e.g., international and operational law advice, fiscal and contract law reviews, the provision of claims, criminal law, and legal assistance services), the specific tasks performed within each of those functional capabilities differ in purpose and scope depending on the level of military operations and the organization performing them. To ensure unity of effort, both the joint force commander (JFC) and the joint force staff judge advocate (SJA) must have a common understanding of who is responsible for performing which legal tasks at each level of military operations and how those tasks are performed. This chapter describes the functions, duties, and responsibilities of the legal organizations within DOD that directly support joint military operations. Figure I-1 depicts the broad relationships of DOD legal organizations to the levels of military operations. These legal organizations may and often do deal with issues above and below their respective levels.

2. General Counsel of the Department of Defense

a. Established by Title 10, United States Code (USC), Section 140, the General Counsel (GC) of DOD is a civilian appointed by the President with the advice and consent of the Senate who serves as the chief legal officer of DOD. The DOD GC provides legal advice to the Secretary and Deputy Secretary of Defense on all legal matters and services performed within, or involving, DOD. In general, the DOD GC is responsible for overseeing all DOD legal services, establishing policy and overseeing the DOD Standards of Conduct Program, establishing DOD policy and positions on specific legal issues, and advising on significant international law issues, including those raised in major military operations, the DOD Law of War Program, and legality of weapons reviews.

b. The DOD GC coordinates and promotes cooperation and mutual understanding among DOD components and between DOD and other government agencies on issues ranging from mergers and acquisitions involving defense suppliers, to significant litigation in which the Department of Justice represents DOD interests. The DOD GC acts as lead counsel in international negotiations conducted by DOD, and maintains the

NOTIONAL RELATIONSHIPS OF DEPARTMENT OF DEFENSE LEGAL ORGANIZATIONS SUPPORTING MILITARY OPERATIONS

DEPARTMENT OF DEFENSE (DOD) LEGAL ORGANIZATIONS	Strategic	Operational	Tactical
DOD General Counsel	X		
Chairman's Legal Counsel	X		
General Counsel of Combat Support Agencies	X		
General Counsel and Judge Advocates General of the Military Departments	X		
Combatant Commander's Staff Judge Advocate (SJA) (Geographic)	X	X	
Combatant Commander's SJA (Functional)	X	X	
Subunified Command SJA	X	X	X
Joint Task Force SJA		X	X
Functional Component SJA		X	X
Service Component SJA		X	X

Figure I-1. Notional Relationships of Department of Defense Legal Organizations Supporting Military Operations

central repository for all DOD-negotiated international agreements. The DOD GC serves as the Director of the Defense Legal Services Agency and, on an informal basis, participates in interagency working groups as necessary to address legal matters affecting more than one department/agency of the US Government.

c. The DOD GC is authorized to issue DOD instructions and other DOD publications that implement policies approved by the Secretary of Defense (SecDef) in the functions assigned to the GC. The DOD GC is responsible for supervision of the general counsels of all DOD agencies and combat support agencies. The DOD GC communicates directly with the heads of the DOD components, other government agencies, representatives of the legislative branch, and members of the public to carry out assigned functions. Communications with the combatant commanders (CCDRs) are transmitted through the Chairman of the Joint Chiefs of Staff (CJCS) unless otherwise directed by the President or SecDef.

3. **General Counsel of Combat Support Agencies**

There are 15 DOD agencies and seven DOD field activities that operate under the authority, direction, and control of the SecDef. These organizations provide support and services in specified functional areas to the combatant commands and the rest of DOD. DOD agencies perform selected support and service functions on a DOD-wide basis. DOD agencies that are assigned wartime support missions are designated as combat support agencies. There are seven combat support agencies: the Defense Intelligence Agency (DIA), the Defense Information Systems Agency, the Defense Contract Management Agency, the Defense Logistics Agency, the National Geospatial-Intelligence Agency, the National Security Agency, and the Defense Threat Reduction Agency (DTRA). DOD field activities perform support and service functions of a more limited scope than DOD agencies.

4. **Legal Counsel, Office of the Chairman of the Joint Chiefs of Staff**

a. Title 10, USC, Section 156 establishes the position of the Legal Counsel (LC) to the CJCS. The officer selected for appointment to serve as LC to the CJCS is recommended by a board of officers convened by SecDef and is appointed by the President from officers of the Judge Advocate General's Corps of one of the military Services, with the advice and consent of the Senate. The LC is appointed in the regular grade of no less than brigadier general or rear admiral (lower half), as appropriate. The LC advises the CJCS, Vice CJCS, joint directors, and Joint Staff on the full spectrum of legal issues. Given the CJCS role as spokesman for the CCDRs, the LC frequently advises and assists the CCDRs' legal staffs. As directed by CJCS, the LC represents the CJCS in the US interagency process, and in coordination with the respective geographic CCDR's SJA, in discussions and negotiations with foreign governments and nongovernmental organizations (NGOs).

b. The LC's Office is staffed with judge advocates from each Service. The areas of practice are varied but are heavily weighted in the areas of operational and international law. Within those areas, the LC is responsible for the following:

(1) Review and advise on rules of engagement (ROE) and the rules for the use of force (RUF); deployment orders and command relationships for military operations; the law of war (often called law of armed conflict [LOAC]); information, special, and counterdrug operations; critical infrastructure protection; combating terrorism, force protection, and detainee issues; and intelligence law and oversight.

(2) Review operation plans and operation plans in concept format for legal sufficiency and accuracy; draft and coordinate required notifications, including reports required by the War Powers Resolution.

(3) Provide counsel and negotiating support for treaties and international agreements, including agreements on status of forces, basing and defense cooperation, arms control, acquisition and cross-servicing, information security, information release, and personnel and unit exchanges.

(4) Render advice on pending legislation affecting joint operations and congressional testimony of the CJCS and Vice CJCS, joint directors, and CCDRs.

(5) Review legality of weapons evaluations as member of the DOD Compliance Review Group; address chemical, biological, radiological, nuclear, and high-yield explosives weapons issues; and review joint doctrine and military-to-military contacts and exercise programs.

(6) Other areas of practice include fiscal law and contracting, law of the sea and oceans policy, air and space law, military justice, administrative law, standards of conduct, litigation coordination, joint personnel, environmental law, Freedom of Information Act and Privacy Act, civil support and consequence management missions, and security and policy reviews.

See Joint Publication (JP) 3-28, Civil Support, *JP 3-27,* Homeland Defense, *and JP 3-08,* Interorganizational Coordination During Joint Operations, *for more detailed guidance.*

5. Military Departments

The GCs of the Military Departments, the judge advocates general (TJAGs), and judge advocates general (JAGs) of the Services provide advice to the Secretaries of the Military Departments and Chiefs of the Services as they carry out their Title 10, USC, responsibilities for organizing, training, and equipping US military forces. Although the Military Departments are not part of the operational chain of command for joint US military operations, their GCs and TJAG/JAGs can provide joint force SJAs with significant reachback capabilities and expertise in international and operational law. TJAG/JAGs also have statutory authority to supervise the administration of military justice within the Services.

a. **General Counsel, Department of the Army (DA).** Title 10, USC, Section 3019 establishes the position of GC of the DA. The GC, DA, is a civilian appointed by the President by and with the advice and consent of the Senate. The GC, DA, is the chief legal officer of the Army who serves as legal counsel to the Secretary of the Army, Under Secretary of the Army, five assistant secretaries, and other members of the Army Secretariat. The GC, DA, also exercises technical supervision over the Office of the

Judge Advocate General, the Office of the Command Counsel, Army Materiel Command, and the Office of the Chief Counsel, Corps of Engineers.

b. **The Judge Advocate General of the Army.** Title 10, USC, Section 3037 establishes the position of TJAG of the Army. TJAG is appointed by the President, by and with the advice and consent of the Senate, from officers of the Judge Advocate General's Corps, who are recommended by the Secretary of the Army. TJAG is appointed in the regular grade of no less than lieutenant general. TJAG is the military legal advisor to the Secretary of the Army and members of the Secretariat in coordination with the Army GC, and is the legal advisor to the Chief of Staff, US Army, and members of the Army Staff. In addition to other duties prescribed by law, policy, and regulation, TJAG is responsible for the technical supervision of members of the Army Judge Advocate General's Corps in the performance of their duties. TJAG also receives the results of proceedings of courts of inquiry and military commissions.

c. **General Counsel, Department of the Navy (DON).** Title 10, USC, Section 5019 establishes the position of GC of the Department of the Navy. The GC, DON, is a civilian appointed by the President by and with the advice and consent of the Senate. The GC, DON, is the principal legal advisor to the Secretary of the Navy and performs such functions as the Secretary of the Navy may prescribe.

d. **The Judge Advocate General of the Navy.** Title 10, USC, Section 5148 establishes the position of TJAG of the Navy. TJAG is appointed by the President, by and with the advice and consent of the Senate, from judge advocates of the Navy or the Marine Corps, who are recommended by the Secretary of the Navy. TJAG is appointed in the regular grade of no less than vice admiral or lieutenant general, as appropriate. In addition to other duties prescribed by law, TJAG, under the direction of the Secretary of the Navy:

(1) Performs duties relating to legal matters arising in the DON as may be assigned.

(2) Performs the functions and duties and exercises the powers prescribed for TJAG in Title 10, USC, Chapter 47.

(3) Receives, revises, and has recorded the proceedings of boards for the examination of officers of the naval service for promotion and retirement.

(4) Performs such other duties as may be assigned.

e. **Counsel for the Commandant of the Marine Corps.** The Counsel for the Commandant of the Marine Corps is responsible for providing to the Commandant of the Marine Corps all legal services that the Navy GC provides to the Navy. The Counsel for the Commandant of the Marine Corps is appointed by the Secretary of the Navy upon joint recommendation of the Navy GC and the Commandant of the Marine Corps. The

Counsel reports directly to the Commandant of the Marine Corps and to the Secretary of the Navy via the Navy GC.

f. **Staff Judge Advocate to the Commandant of the Marine Corps.** Title 10, USC, Section 5046 establishes the position of the SJA to the Commandant of the Marine Corps. An officer of the Marine Corps who is a judge advocate is detailed as SJA to the Commandant of the Marine Corps. The SJA is the legal advisor to the Commandant of the Marine Corps on legal matters, administrative law, operational law, and legal assistance matters. The SJA is also the Director of the Judge Advocate Division, Headquarters, US Marine Corps, and thereby provides supervision and management of the Military Law; Operational Law; Research and Civil Law; Legal Assistance; Judge Advocate Support; and Information, Plans, and Programs branches of the Judge Advocate Division, and of the Chief Defense Counsel of the Marine Corps. The SJA is appointed in the regular grade of major general.

g. **General Counsel, Department of the Air Force (DAF).** Title 10, USC, Section 8019 establishes the position of GC of the DAF. The GC, DAF, is a civilian appointed by the President by and with the advice and consent of the Senate. The GC performs such functions as the Secretary of the Air Force (SECAF) may prescribe. The relationship between the General Counsel and TJAG is unique. Both officials are legal advisors to the Secretary and the Chief of Staff of the Air Force with right of independent access and have the ability to provide independent legal advice to those officials. This is accomplished through two staff organizations that must be independent of each other. Both officials provide legal opinions that are authoritative for the Air Force.

h. **The Judge Advocate General of the Air Force.** Title 10, USC, Section 8037 establishes the position of TJAG of the Air Force. TJAG is appointed by the President, by and with the advice and consent of the Senate, from judge advocates of the Air Force. TJAG is appointed in the regular grade of no less than lieutenant general. In addition to other duties prescribed by law, TJAG:

(1) Serves as the legal advisor of the SECAF and of all officers and agencies of the DAF;

(2) Directs the officers of the Air Force designated as judge advocates in the performance of their duties; and

(3) Receives, revises, and has recorded the proceedings of courts of inquiry and military commissions.

i. **The Judge Advocate General of the Coast Guard.** The Homeland Security Act amended the Uniform Code of Military Justice to afford the new Secretary of Homeland Security the discretion to designate any official to serve as TJAG of the Coast Guard. TJAG of the Coast Guard is designated by the Secretary of Homeland Security. The designated individual serves in the capacity as TJAG of the US Coast Guard, except when the Coast Guard is operating as a service of the Department of the Navy under Title

14, USC, Section 2. TJAG is the principal legal advisor to the Commandant of the Coast Guard and oversees the administration of military justice for the Coast Guard. The Coast Guard TJAG is an officer of the Coast Guard who serves in the grade of rear admiral.

j. **Chief Counsel, National Guard Bureau (NGB).** The Chief Counsel, NGB provides legal services, advice, and opinions to the Chief, NGB; the Director of the NGB Joint Staff; the Directors of the Army and Air National Guard and their respective staffs; state adjutants general; full-time state judge advocates; United States property and fiscal officers; DOD offices and other federal and state agencies. The Chief Counsel also liaises with other legal offices within DOD and other federal and state agencies.

6. **Joint Force Staff Judge Advocate**

a. The joint force SJA (also titled "the judge advocate" or "command judge advocate") is the principal legal advisor to the JFC and a key member of a JFC's personal staff. The joint force SJA is the principal legal advisor to the CCDR, deputy commander, and chief of staff, and they coordinate as necessary with the legal staff of the other combatant commands. A combatant command SJA coordinates, as necessary, with the legal staffs at the Office of the Secretary of Defense, Joint Chiefs of Staff (JCS), and the Military Departments. The joint force SJA reports directly to the JFC. In the contemporary operating environment, the joint force SJA provides the full spectrum of legal support through direct and reachback capability to joint operations across the range of military operations. Figure I-2 depicts where the SJA fits in a typical joint force command.

b. In addition to the authorities vested in SJAs by Title 10, USC, Chapter 47 (Uniform Code of Military Justice), the joint force SJA issues coordinating guidance on legal matters to subordinate components under the authority of the JFC to optimize legal support to the joint force. Services and Service components retain authority for providing legal support to their forces, subject to the coordinating guidance of the joint force SJA.

c. **SJAs at Levels of Joint Forces.** Joint forces are established at three levels: combatant commands, subordinate unified commands, and joint task forces (JTFs). Joint force judge advocates provide legal support at each of these levels. Each level addresses unique legal issues and has a specific legal basis for assigning responsibilities, establishing or delegating appropriate command relationships, and establishing coordinating instructions between joint forces commands and their components.

(1) **Combatant Command SJA.** The combatant command SJA is a judge advocate selected by the CCDR from among those officers nominated for the position by each of the Military Services. The combatant command SJA serves as counsel for the command, providing legal advice to the CCDR and combatant command staff on the full spectrum of legal issues, with varied emphasis depending upon the combatant command's mission, force structure, and whether it has a geographic or functional responsibility. The combatant command SJA exercises technical supervision over the administration of command legal services within that combatant command. The

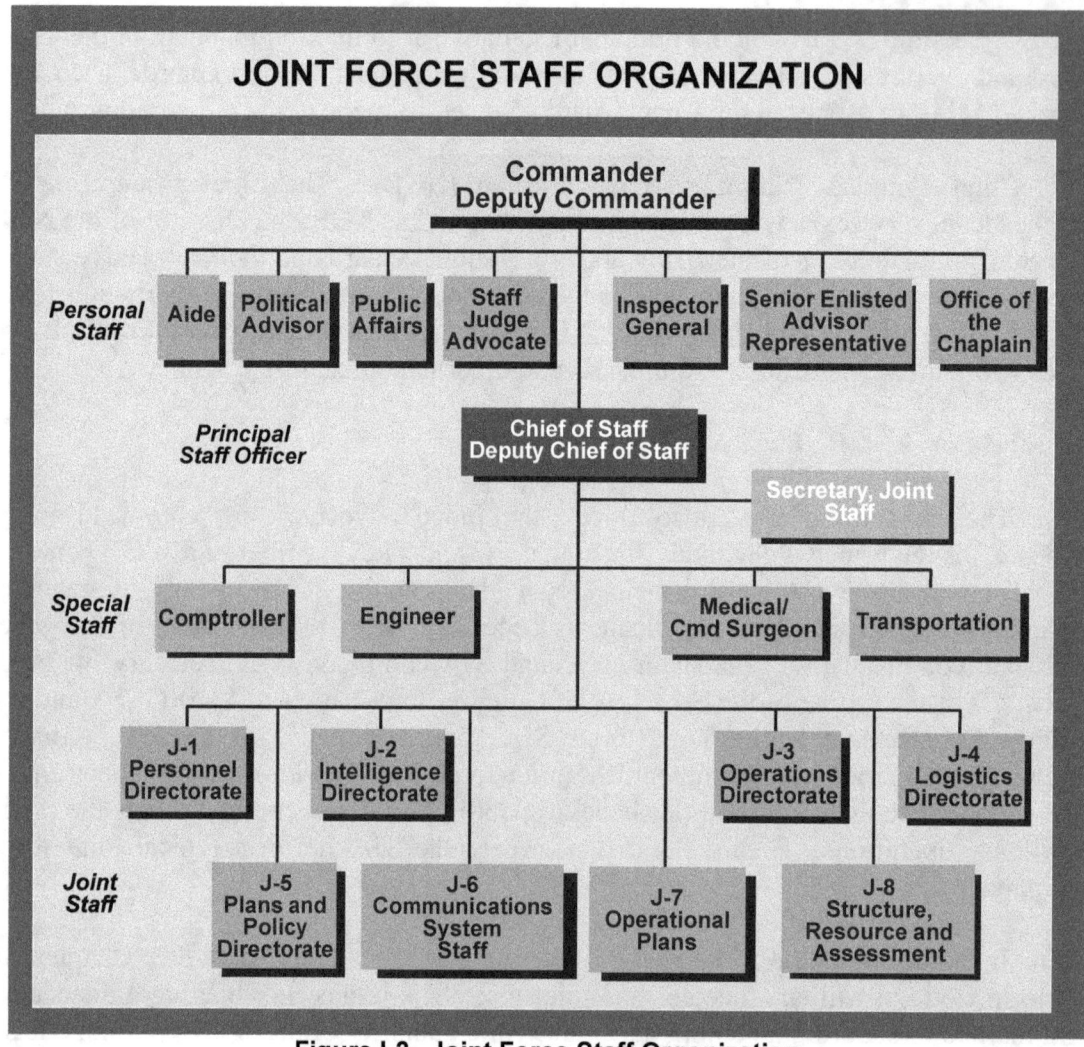

Figure I-2. Joint Force Staff Organization

combatant command SJA reviews the legal support capabilities available in the combatant command and recommends allocation of legal resources to support the combatant command missions most effectively and to prevent or eliminate the unnecessary duplication and overlap of functions among supporting legal organizations. The combatant command SJA also oversees the collection of legal lessons learned from supporting SJAs and the distribution of legal lessons learned to joint and Service repositories.

(a) **Geographic Combatant Commands.** The joint force SJAs supporting the six geographic combatant commands: (United States Africa Command; United States Northern Command; United States Central Command; United States European Command; United States Pacific Command; and United States Southern Command) provide the full spectrum of legal services with both a strategic and operational emphasis. The areas of practice mirror those addressed by CJCS/LC detailed in paragraph 4 above, with a greater focus on joint operational law issues pertaining to their commander's geographic area of responsibility (AOR). They also supervise legal aspects of the theater security cooperation programs within their AORs and oversee the provision of legal services within subordinate unified commands, JTFs, and functional and Service components.

(b) **Functional Combatant Commands**

1. The joint force SJAs of the three functional combatant commands (United States Transportation Command [USTRANSCOM], United States Strategic Command [USSTRATCOM], and United States Special Operations Command [USSOCOM]) similarly provide the full spectrum of legal services, but also have legal responsibilities related to the combatant command's particular functional areas.

2. The USTRANSCOM SJA provides legal expertise in its core functional competency of transportation law for USTRANSCOM and DOD. Specifically, the USTRANSCOM SJA focuses on transportation acquisition, fiscal, international, personnel, military justice, operations, intellectual property, civil, administrative and environmental law, and transportation-related insurance law.

3. The USSTRATCOM SJA provides legal advice to support the USSTRATCOM missions related to strategic deterrence operations; freedom of action in space and cyberspace; integrated lethal and nonlethal capabilities in support of US JFCs; synchronization of global missile defense and combating weapons of mass destruction plans and operations; and intelligence, surveillance, and reconnaissance. In particular, the USSTRATCOM SJA focuses on international and operational law in the areas of cyberspace, space, and targeting, as well as administrative law, fiscal law, and military justice.

4. The USSOCOM SJA provides legal advice on issues involving special operations forces (SOF). In addition to the command authority inherent in a combatant command, the Commander, USSOCOM has Service-like responsibilities for SOF pursuant to Title 10, USC, Section 167 and maintains a particular emphasis on pursuing overseas contingency operations.

(2) **Subordinate Unified Command SJA.** When assigned to a subordinate unified command (subunified command), an SJA serves as the primary legal advisor to that command. The subunified SJA receives guidance from the combatant command SJA and may have certain functional legal areas performed by the combatant command SJA (e.g., contract law). If the subunified command does not have direct legal support, the combatant command SJA typically provides those services to the subunified command.

For a more detailed discussion of combatant command, subordinate unified command, and JTF organizations, responsibilities, and functions, see JP 1, Doctrine for the Armed Forces of the United States, *and JP 3-0,* Joint Operations.

(3) **Joint Task Force SJAs.** The most common type of joint force command established to accomplish a specific mission in a geographic area or perform a particular function is the JTF. The JTF SJA is the principal legal advisor to the commander, JTF

(CJTF) and is an integral part of the JTF staff. The JTF SJA provides support to multiple JTF boards, centers, and cells that require legal expertise in the planning and employment of JTF forces. The training, equipping, and organization of legal personnel assigned or attached to the JTF headquarters (HQ) falls to the JTF SJA. The JTF SJA develops the legal estimate during planning and recommends requirements for the JTF joint manning document (JMD). By task organizing, the JTF SJA ensures the SJA section is balanced as to numbers, experience, influence of position, and rank of component, allied, and coalition members of the operation. Ideally, the SJA section will reflect the composition of the JTF and character of the operation. The JTF SJA coordinates with the supported combatant command SJA and the supporting component SJAs to optimize legal support to the JTF. The JTF SJA will be discussed in detail in Chapter III, "Legal Support to the Joint Task Force."

For a more detailed discussion of JTF, see JP 3-33, Joint Task Force Headquarters.

d. **Functional Components.** Component command SJAs, like JTF SJAs, are the principal legal command advisors to the commander and provide legal support to multiple boards, centers, and cells. The functional component SJA coordinates with the combatant command SJA.

e. **Service Components.** Joint force commands include Service components. Service component command SJAs advise the Service component commander on issues that are service specific. In addition, the component SJA coordinates and receives guidance from the combatant command or JTF SJA on all matters that relate to the component command's supporting mission.

f. **Reserve Component Support.** Most joint force commands include judge advocates from one or more units of the Reserve Component (RC) (i.e., the Army Reserve, the Army National Guard of the United States, the Navy Reserve, the Marine Corps Reserve, the Air National Guard of the United States, the Air Force Reserve, and the Coast Guard Reserve). Reserve judge advocates mobilized to support an operation always serve in a Title 10, USC, status and are trained to fulfill both short-term and long-term legal requirements for the command. However, because the status of Army National Guard and Air National Guard judge advocates may change, they may be subject to differing manning requirements. It is important that the joint force SJA work with the combatant command's RC support office for assistance in assigning or attaching the RC judge advocates to the combatant command or the component commands of the joint force.

g. **Duties and Responsibilities.** The joint force SJA's general duties and responsibilities are shown in Figure I-3. Legal staffs require adequate resources to conduct legal research and perform assigned legal duties. Specific planning considerations are discussed in Chapters II, "Legal Support to Joint Operation Planning," and III, "Legal Support to the Joint Task Force."

JOINT FORCE STAFF JUDGE ADVOCATE'S DUTIES AND RESPONSIBILITIES
Formation, Deployment, and Management of the Legal Staff
Ensure personnel have appropriate security clearance for mission/duties.
Form, deploy, employ, transition, and redeploy the staff judge advocate section.
Train section personnel.
Manage section operations, including information and security.
Requisition and control section resources.
Coordinate the assignment, promotion, transfer, and replacement of section personnel.
Domestic Operations
Know the legal basis for the military operation.
Assist commands with the crafting of rules for the use of force (RUF) and related information papers, memoranda of law, and memoranda of agreement with supported civil authorities.
Advise joint force commander (JFC) and other staff on state and local legal requirements and interagency and interstate agreements that affect the military civil support mission.
Oversee or offer training on Posse Comitatus and the governing legal principles applicable to RUF, including the use of both lethal and nonlethal force, and rules of engagement (ROE). Advise the JFC and other staff on proper duty status for participating personnel, medical credentialing, information operations, fiscal law and contracts, claims, and other pertinent areas of the law.
Planning, Coordination, and Oversight
Prepare the legal considerations paragraph of the base operation plan or order according to Chairman of the Joint Chiefs of Staff Manual (CJCSM) 3122.03C, Joint Operation and Planning Execution System, Vol II: (Planning Formats).
Prepare the legal appendix to the personnel annex of the operation order according to CJCSM 3122.03C, Joint Operation Planning and Execution System, Vol II: (Planning Formats).
Continuously assess mission capability and any strengths or deficiencies in joint legal doctrine, organization, training, materiel, and education.
Serve as single point of contact for all legal issues of joint origin that involve more than one Service or that affect the external relations of the joint force command.
Capture, act on, and share joint legal lessons learned, issues, and key observations from operations, training events, and other sources.
Liaise with counterparts at higher, lower, and adjacent headquarters, Department of Defense (DOD) and other US Government agencies, foreign government agencies, intergovernmental organizations, and nongovernmental organizations, including liaison with the International Committee of the Red Cross.
Advise on issues related to rule of law and military operations.
Maintenance of Good Order and Discipline
Ensure that each Service member is afforded due process and administrative rights.
Coordinate with Service element staff judge advocate or element commander those military justice matters most appropriately handled through Service channels.
Supervise the administration of military justice throughout the joint force.
Recommend standard policies applicable to all Services within the command when necessary to maintain good order and discipline or preserve US-host nation relations (e.g., general orders and black market and currency control regulations).

Figure I-3. Joint Force Staff Judge Advocate's Duties and Responsibilities

JOINT FORCE STAFF JUDGE ADVOCATE'S DUTIES AND RESPONSIBILITIES (cont'd)
Maintenance of Good Order and Discipline (cont'd)
Recommend uniform policies and procedures for requesting joint command courts-martial convening authority, exercising disciplinary authority over members of other Services, and creating Service units within the joint force headquarters and subordinate joint force headquarters.
Communicate directly with the JFC on military justice matters, to include advising on appropriate disposition of charges before referral to trial by courts-martial and recommending appropriate convening authorities action on courts-martial.
Status of Forces and Relations with Host Nation
Support negotiation and conclusion of international agreements, including acquisition and cross-servicing agreements, status-of-forces agreements (SOFAs), and status of mission agreements, in accordance with DOD Directive (DODD) 5530.3, International Agreements.
Advise the JFC and staff concerning assertions of foreign criminal jurisdiction over military personnel and civilians accompanying the force.
Monitor relations with governments and inhabitants of foreign countries.
Law of War and Related International Legal Considerations
Ensure that all plans, orders, policies, ROE, and target lists issued by the command and its subordinate commands are reviewed by legal advisors for compliance with applicable law and policy as required by DODD 2311.01E, DOD Law of War Program, and Chairman of the Joint Chiefs of Staff Instruction (CJCSI) 5810.01C, Implementation of DOD Law of War Program.
Assist the J-3 or J-5 in preparing ROE request and authorization messages according to CJCSI 3121.01B, Standing Rules of Engagement/Standing Rules for the Use of Force for US Forces.
Monitor conduct of war crimes trials.
Law of War and Related International Legal Considerations (cont'd)
Advise the JFC and staff on the legal authority for, and constraints on, the conduct of military operations, including the use of force; freedom of navigation; overflight of international and national airspace; basing rights; foreign intelligence and counterintelligence activities; information operations; joint targeting; treatment of wounded and sick, prisoners of war, and civilian persons and property, including migrants, refugees, and internally displaced persons; conduct of tribunals under Article 5 of the Third Geneva Convention; governance of occupied enemy territory; exercise of military authority over civilians and private property in the United States; and storage, transportation, and use of chemical, biological, radiological, nuclear, or high-yield explosives, and other weapons subject to special restrictions.
Contractor Personnel Integration
Ensure that all JFC plans and policies are in compliance with US law, international law, local law, SOFAs, and DOD policy as they relate to the use of contracted, vice military, support. Specific concerns are legal status of US and third country national contractor personnel hired outside of the operational area; force protection/security measures; and, arming contractor personnel (includes arming for self-defense and for security support). See DOD Instruction (DODI) 3020.41, Contractor Personnel Authorized to Accompany the US Armed Forces.
Advise the JFC and staff on contract law matters, i.e., the application of domestic and international law to acquire goods, services, and construction. Specifically, battlefield acquisition, contingency contracting, bid protests and contract dispute litigation, procurement fraud oversight, commercial activities, and acquisition and cross-servicing agreements.

Figure I-3. Joint Force Staff Judge Advocate's Duties and Responsibilities (cont'd)

JOINT FORCE STAFF JUDGE ADVOCATE'S DUTIES AND RESPONSIBILITIES (cont'd)
Reporting
Monitor and advise the JFC and staff concerning investigation and disposition of significant incidents required to be reported via operation report 3-PINNACLE and other flagword reports (e.g., grave breaches of the law of war, asylum incidents, aircraft accidents, and possible border violations). See CJCSM 3150.03B, Joint Reporting Structure Event and Incident Reports. Report Law of War violations in accordance with DODD 2311.01E, DOD Law of War Program.
Submit legal status reports.
Provision of Legal Services
Man joint boards, bureaus, centers, cells, and working groups.
Monitor and coordinate the provision of legal services throughout the command.
Record significant activities.
Provide legal advice to investigating officers, review their reports for legal sufficiency, and make appropriate recommendations to the appointing and/or approving authority.
Provide legal assistance to the JFC and staff.
Arrange for the provision of claims, trial defense, trial judiciary, and other legal services as appropriate to the JFC and staff.
Advise the JFC and staff concerning legal issues related to provision of logistic support to non-DOD entities.
Advise the JFC and staff concerning transfers or other disposition of military property.
Advise the JFC and staff concerning acquisition or disposition of real property, goods, services, and other contingency contracting issues.
Monitor accountability for loss, damage, or destruction of military property.
Advise the JFC and staff concerning legal issues related to military personnel matters, including mobilization, military status, pay, allowances, promotion, reduction, separation, authorized activities, conscientious objector applications, and complaints under Article 138, Uniform Code of Military Justice.
Recommend policy for accounting for captured weapons, war trophies, documents, and equipment.
Advise the JFC and staff concerning civilian personnel matters, including deployment issues, adverse action appeals to the Merit Systems Protection Board, equal employment opportunity discrimination complaints, grievance arbitrations, negotiation of union labor agreements, unfair labor practice hearings and grievance arbitrations, and unfair labor practice complaints and negotiability disputes before the Federal Labor Relations Authority.
Advise the JFC and staff concerning requests for political asylum and temporary refuge.
Provide advice on funding of military operations and the obligation and expenditure of appropriated funds. For example, provide counsel concerning solatia payments and Commander Emergency Response Program funds.
Ensure compliance with applicable environmental laws and policies.
Advise the JFC and staff concerning standards of conduct issues, including giving and accepting gifts, filing financial disclosure reports, and post-government service employment restrictions.
Serve as ethics advisor.

Figure I-3. Joint Force Staff Judge Advocate's Duties and Responsibilities (cont'd)

JOINT FORCE STAFF JUDGE ADVOCATE'S DUTIES AND RESPONSIBILITIES (cont'd)
Provision of Legal Services (cont'd)
Advise commanders on investigations. Provide legal advice to investigating officers, review their reports for legal sufficiency, and make appropriate recommendations to the appointing and/or approving authority.
Advise the JTF commander on command responsibility and accountability.
Supervise investigation and processing of claims arising from activities of the JFC and staff under the Military Claims Act, Federal Tort Claims Act, Foreign Claims Act, Personnel Claims Act, reciprocal international agreements (e.g., SOFA claims), Suits in Admiralty Act, Public Vessels Act, and other applicable statutes, as well as assignment of claims responsibilities in accordance with DODI 5515.08.
Provide legal assistance, i.e., provide personal civil legal services to Service members, their family members, and other eligible personnel.
Aspects of intelligence law exist in all operations. It is imperative that judge advocates consider them when planning and reviewing both operations in general and intelligence operations in particular.
Perform other duties assigned by the JFC.
Training
Provide training to the JFC and staff on the law of war, ROE, standing and general orders issued by the commander, foreign law, ethics, procurement integrity, and other subjects as required and appropriate.
Provide training concerning status of US forces in foreign countries.

Figure I-3. Joint Force Staff Judge Advocate's Duties and Responsibilities (cont'd)

CHAPTER II
LEGAL SUPPORT TO JOINT OPERATION PLANNING

"Strategic and tactical planning must be completely unified, combat forces organized into unified commands, each equipped with the most efficient weapons systems that science can develop, singly led and prepared to fight as one, regardless of Service."

34th President Dwight Eisenhower, (1953-1961)

1. Introduction

a. Legal advisors within DOD perform a wide variety of planning tasks at the strategic, operational, and tactical levels. They support their organizations in carrying out their planning responsibilities by providing legal advice on the myriad of regulations, laws, policies, treaties, and agreements that apply to joint military operations. Legal advisors actively participate in the entire planning process from joint intelligence preparation of the operational environment development, to mission analysis, to course of action (COA) development and recommendation, through execution. Strategic and operational planning typically occurs at the JTF and higher echelons. Legal advisors who perform planning tasks at the tactical level typically do so as a Service component of a JTF. Planning at that level often involves a single Service that follows Service doctrine, using tactics, techniques, and procedures contained in Military Department and Service publications.

b. Military planning consists of joint strategic planning with its three subsets: security cooperation planning, joint operation planning, and force planning. Legal advisors assist decision makers at every echelon in translating policy decisions into legally acceptable plans and orders that support national security objectives. At the strategic level this is accomplished within the framework of four interrelated defense planning systems and associated processes: the National Security Council System (NSCS), the Planning, Programming, Budgeting, and Execution (PPBE) process, the Joint Strategic Planning System (JSPS), and Adaptive Planning and Execution (APEX) system. At the operational level, planning occurs under the umbrella of APEX and primarily through the joint operation planning process. This chapter describes the role and responsibilities of the legal advisor at each echelon during the strategic and operational joint planning processes.

c. For domestic operations, commanders and their judge advocates must understand DOD normally acts in support of another federal, state, local or tribal government or agency. Judge advocates must work closely with all appropriate organizations and agencies to help the commander stay within the boundaries of law and policy that govern military support in the United States.

2. Law of War Principles

It is DOD policy that members of the DOD Components comply with the law of war during all armed conflicts, however such conflicts are characterized, and in all other military operations. Some of the law of war principles to be considered during the planning process are as follows:

a. **Military Necessity.** The principle of military necessity justifies those measures not forbidden by international law that are indispensable for securing the complete submission of the enemy as soon as possible. However, this principle is not applied in a vacuum. It must be applied in conjunction with other law of war principles. Military necessity generally prohibits the intentional targeting of protected persons (civilians, hostile personnel who have surrendered or are otherwise "out of combat," etc.) and places (objects or places that are used for purely civilian purposes, such as hospitals, schools, and cultural property that have not been converted to or for military/hostile use) because they do not constitute legitimate military objectives in furtherance of the accomplishment of the mission.

b. **Unnecessary Suffering.** The principle of unnecessary suffering forbids the employment of means and methods of warfare calculated to cause unnecessary suffering. This principle acknowledges that combatants' necessary suffering, which may include severe injury and loss of life, is lawful. This principle largely applies to the legality of weapons and ammunition. Generally, weapons and ammunition that have been issued by DOD have been reviewed to ensure compliance with the law of war and this principle. However, approved weapons and ammunition also may not be used in a way that will cause unnecessary suffering or injury. A weapon or munition would be deemed to cause unnecessary suffering if, in its normal use, the injury caused by it is disproportionate to the military necessity for it, that is, the military advantage to be gained from its use.

c. **Distinction.** This principle requires parties to a conflict to distinguish between combatants and noncombatants and to distinguish between military objectives and protected property and places. Parties to a conflict must direct their operations only against military objectives. Military objectives are combatants and those objects which by their nature, location, purpose, or use make an effective contribution to military action and whose total or partial destruction, capture or neutralization, in the circumstances ruling at the time, offer a definitive military advantage.

d. **Proportionality.** The principle of proportionality prohibits attacks that may be expected to cause incidental loss of civilian life, injury to civilians, damage to civilian objects, or a combination thereof, which would be excessive in relation to the concrete and direct military advantage expected to be gained. As such, this principle is only applicable when an attack may possibly affect civilians or civilian objects, and thereby, may cause collateral damage. Proportionality is a way in which a military commander must assess his or her obligations as to the principle of distinction, while avoiding actions that are indiscriminate.

3. Legal Support to Strategic Level Planning

a. The strategic-level planning processes within the NSCS, PPBE, JSPS, and APEX take place primarily between the President and/or SecDef, the CJCS, and the CCDRs. Their legal advisors—the DOD GC, the LC, and the CCDRs' SJAs—plan and coordinate DOD-wide and theater-level legal support for the full range of planning activities including mobilization, deployment, employment, sustainment, redeployment, and demobilization of forces. This paragraph provides an overview of these systems and describes the legal advisor's responsibilities within them.

b. **NSCS.** The NSCS provides the interagency framework for establishing national strategy and policy objectives that ultimately receive Presidential approval. Figure II-1

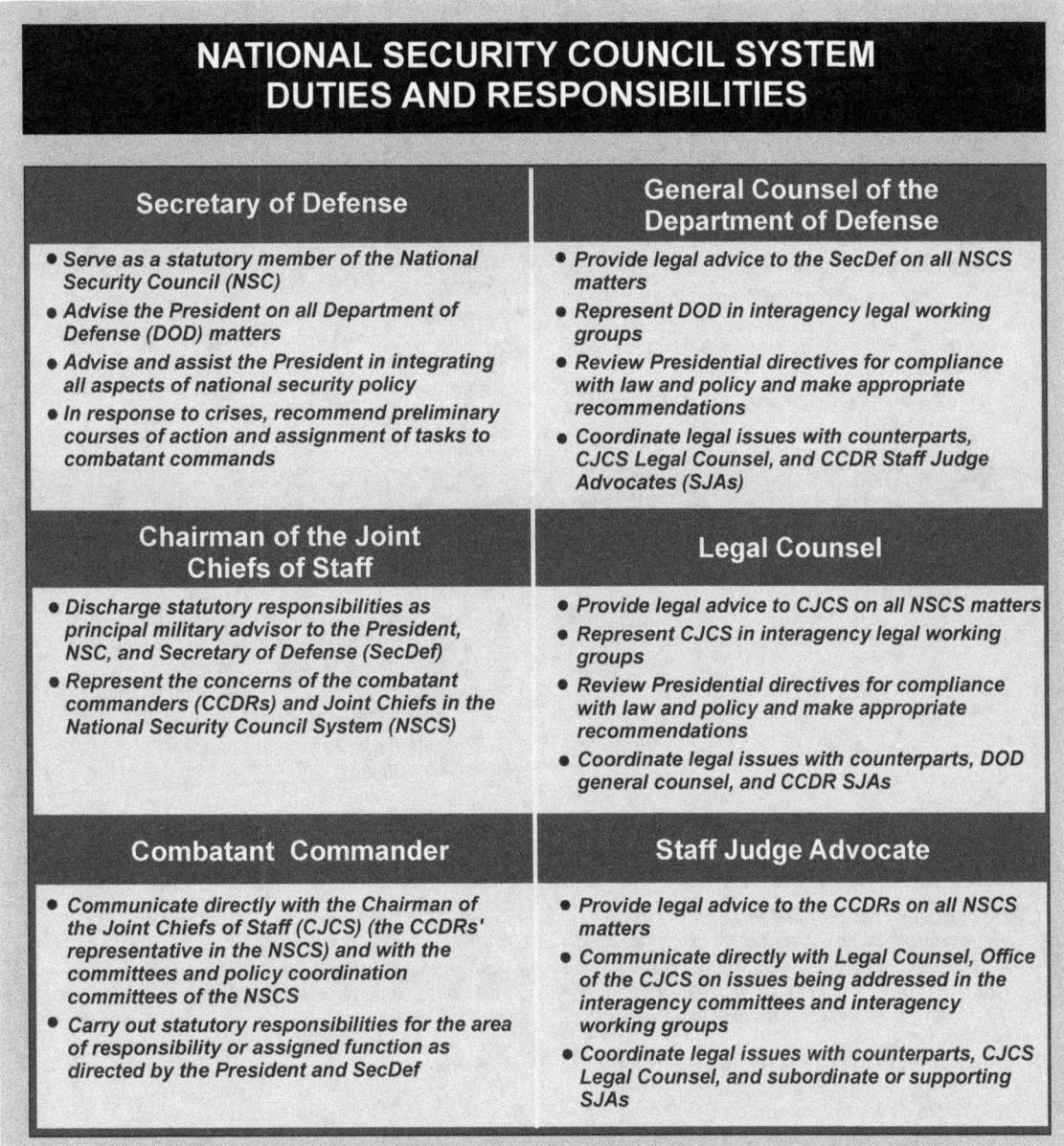

NATIONAL SECURITY COUNCIL SYSTEM DUTIES AND RESPONSIBILITIES

Secretary of Defense

- *Serve as a statutory member of the National Security Council (NSC)*
- *Advise the President on all Department of Defense (DOD) matters*
- *Advise and assist the President in integrating all aspects of national security policy*
- *In response to crises, recommend preliminary courses of action and assignment of tasks to combatant commands*

General Counsel of the Department of Defense

- *Provide legal advice to the SecDef on all NSCS matters*
- *Represent DOD in interagency legal working groups*
- *Review Presidential directives for compliance with law and policy and make appropriate recommendations*
- *Coordinate legal issues with counterparts, CJCS Legal Counsel, and CCDR Staff Judge Advocates (SJAs)*

Chairman of the Joint Chiefs of Staff

- *Discharge statutory responsibilities as principal military advisor to the President, NSC, and Secretary of Defense (SecDef)*
- *Represent the concerns of the combatant commanders (CCDRs) and Joint Chiefs in the National Security Council System (NSCS)*

Legal Counsel

- *Provide legal advice to CJCS on all NSCS matters*
- *Represent CJCS in interagency legal working groups*
- *Review Presidential directives for compliance with law and policy and make appropriate recommendations*
- *Coordinate legal issues with counterparts, DOD general counsel, and CCDR SJAs*

Combatant Commander

- *Communicate directly with the Chairman of the Joint Chiefs of Staff (CJCS) (the CCDRs' representative in the NSCS) and with the committees and policy coordination committees of the NSCS*
- *Carry out statutory responsibilities for the area of responsibility or assigned function as directed by the President and SecDef*

Staff Judge Advocate

- *Provide legal advice to the CCDRs on all NSCS matters*
- *Communicate directly with Legal Counsel, Office of the CJCS on issues being addressed in the interagency committees and interagency working groups*
- *Coordinate legal issues with counterparts, CJCS Legal Counsel, and subordinate or supporting SJAs*

Figure II-1. National Security Council System Duties and Responsibilities

lists the major duties and responsibilities of the SecDef, CJCS, CCDRs, and their legal advisors within the NSCS.

c. **PPBE.** The PPBE is the DOD-wide process that relates resources to strategy. This PPBE objective is the acquisition and allocation of resources to meet the operational requirements of the CCDRs and the provisioning requirements of the Services and combat support agencies. The major duties and responsibilities of the SecDef, CJCS, CCDRs, and their legal advisors within the PPBE are listed in Figure II-2.

d. **JSPS.** The JSPS is one of the primary means by which the CJCS, in coordination with the other members of the JCS and the CCDRs, accomplishes contingency planning and provides military advice to the President and SecDef and recommendations to the PPBE.

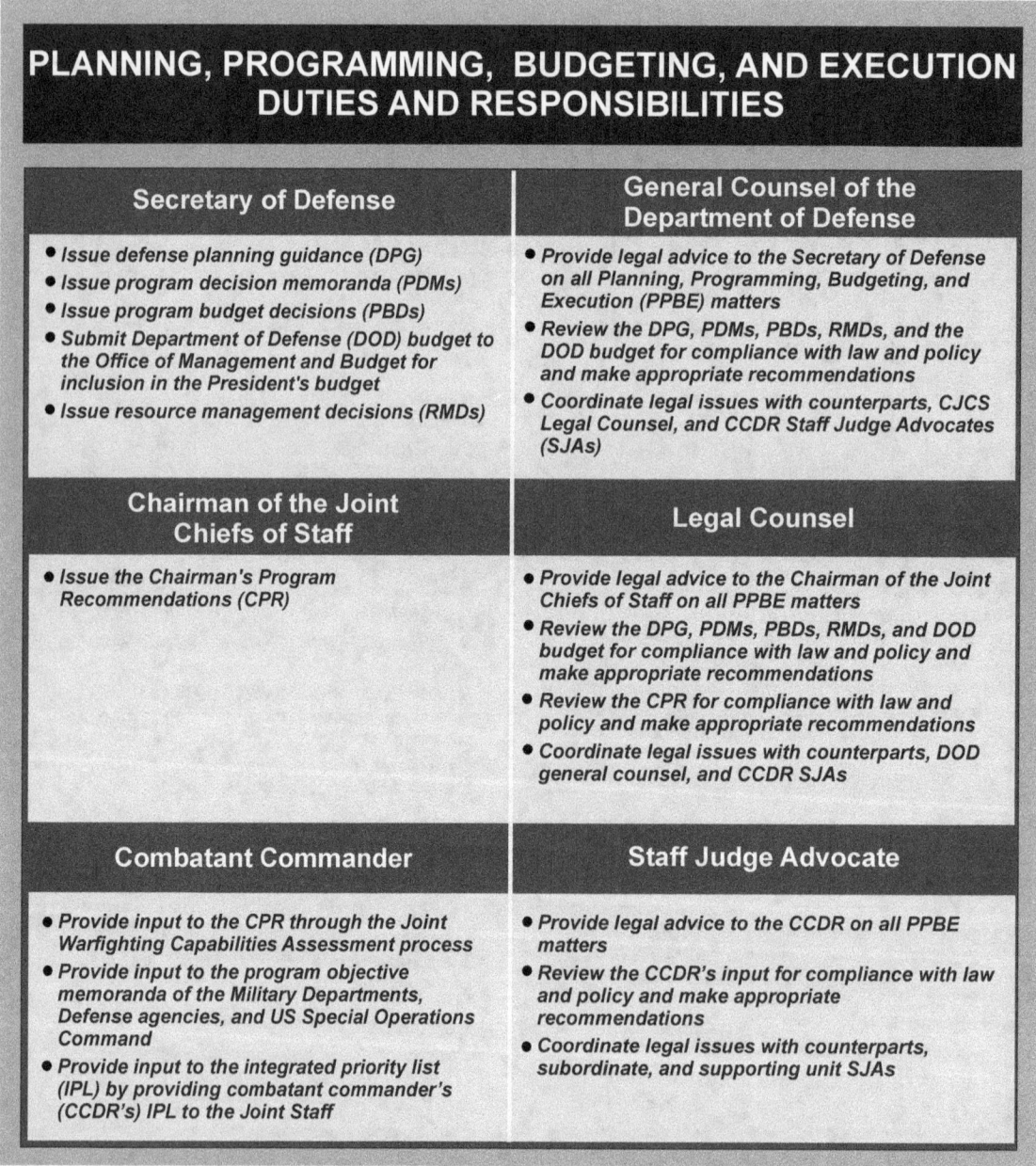

PLANNING, PROGRAMMING, BUDGETING, AND EXECUTION DUTIES AND RESPONSIBILITIES

Secretary of Defense

- *Issue defense planning guidance (DPG)*
- *Issue program decision memoranda (PDMs)*
- *Issue program budget decisions (PBDs)*
- *Submit Department of Defense (DOD) budget to the Office of Management and Budget for inclusion in the President's budget*
- *Issue resource management decisions (RMDs)*

General Counsel of the Department of Defense

- *Provide legal advice to the Secretary of Defense on all Planning, Programming, Budgeting, and Execution (PPBE) matters*
- *Review the DPG, PDMs, PBDs, RMDs, and the DOD budget for compliance with law and policy and make appropriate recommendations*
- *Coordinate legal issues with counterparts, CJCS Legal Counsel, and CCDR Staff Judge Advocates (SJAs)*

Chairman of the Joint Chiefs of Staff

- *Issue the Chairman's Program Recommendations (CPR)*

Legal Counsel

- *Provide legal advice to the Chairman of the Joint Chiefs of Staff on all PPBE matters*
- *Review the DPG, PDMs, PBDs, RMDs, and DOD budget for compliance with law and policy and make appropriate recommendations*
- *Review the CPR for compliance with law and policy and make appropriate recommendations*
- *Coordinate legal issues with counterparts, DOD general counsel, and CCDR SJAs*

Combatant Commander

- *Provide input to the CPR through the Joint Warfighting Capabilities Assessment process*
- *Provide input to the program objective memoranda of the Military Departments, Defense agencies, and US Special Operations Command*
- *Provide input to the integrated priority list (IPL) by providing combatant commander's (CCDR's) IPL to the Joint Staff*

Staff Judge Advocate

- *Provide legal advice to the CCDR on all PPBE matters*
- *Review the CCDR's input for compliance with law and policy and make appropriate recommendations*
- *Coordinate legal issues with counterparts, subordinate, and supporting unit SJAs*

Figure II-2. Planning, Programming, Budgeting, and Execution Duties and Responsibilities

JSPS products—such as the National Military Strategy and the Joint Strategic Capabilities Plan—provide guidance and instructions on military policy, strategy, plans, forces, and resource requirements and allocations essential to successful execution of the National Security Strategy and other Presidential directives. Figure II-3 details the major duties and responsibilities of the SecDef, CJCS, CCDRs, and their legal advisors within the JSPS.

e. **APEX.** Joint operation planning is accomplished through the APEX system. The joint planning and execution community uses APEX to monitor, plan, and execute mobilization, deployment, employment, sustainment, redeployment, and demobilization activities associated with joint operations. Clear strategic guidance and frequent interaction between senior leaders and planners promote early understanding of, and agreement on, planning assumptions, considerations, risks, and other key factors. Legal advisors participate at all stages of this adaptive and collaborative planning system.

(1) **Deliberate planning** takes place primarily at the strategic level between the CJCS and the supported CCDR. Figure II-4 lists by phase the major duties and

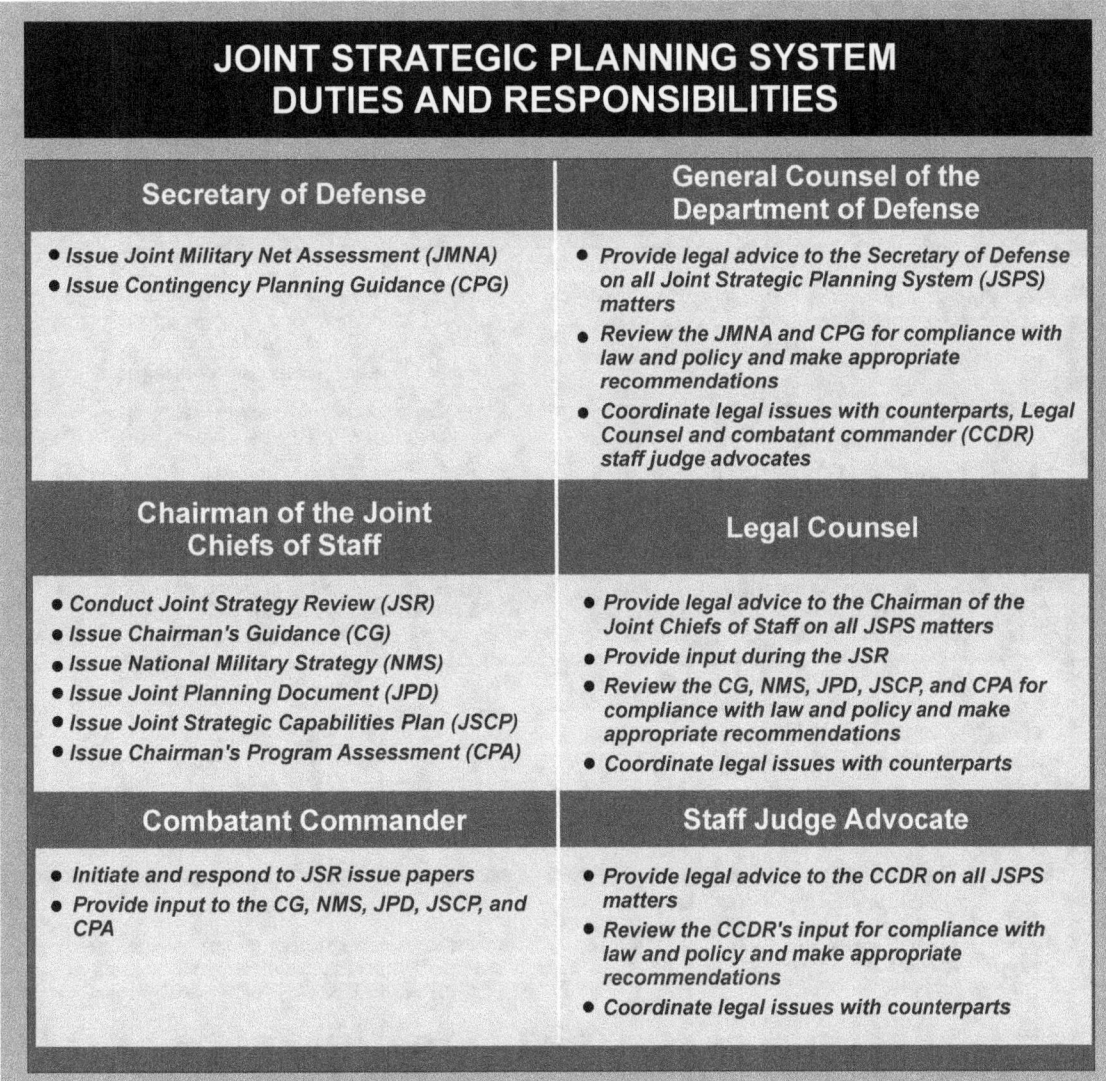

Figure II-3. Joint Strategic Planning System Duties and Responsibilities

responsibilities of the CJCS, CCDRs, and their legal advisors within the joint planning process.

(2) **Crisis action planning (CAP)** procedures are used to plan for and execute military operations in time-sensitive and imminent crisis situations. Legal counsel advises at each phase of CAP as the process adapts to accommodate the dynamic requirements of changing events. Figure II-5 highlights the key responsibilities of legal advisors at the DOD, Joint Staff, and supported combatant commands in the initial phases

ADAPTIVE PLANNING AND EXECUTION SYSTEM DELIBERATE PLANNING DUTIES AND RESPONSIBILITIES

Chairman of the Joint Chiefs of Staff	Legal Counsel
Activity I, Initiation Joint Strategic Capabilities Plan • *Assign planning tasks to supported combatant commanders* • *Specify the types of plans required* • *Apportion forces and resources* • *Issue planning guidance*	**Activity I, Initiation Joint Strategic Capabilities Plan** • *Review planning documents* • *Review applicable laws, policies, treaties, and agreements*
Activity II, Concept Development • *Review and approve the supported combatant commander's strategic concept*	**Activity II, Concept Development** • *Review the combatant commander's strategic concept for compliance with law and policy and make appropriate recommendations* • *Coordinate legal issues with counterparts*
Activity III, Plan Development • *Assist the supported combatant commander*	**Activity III, Plan Development** • *Assist the supported combatant command staff judge advocate*
Activity IV, Plan Review • *In coordination with the Joint Chiefs of Staff, Services, and Department of Defense agencies, assess and validate the supported combatant commander's operation plan (OPLAN) and time-phased force and deployment data using criteria of adequacy, feasibility, acceptability, and compliance with joint doctrine* • *Approve or disapprove the OPLAN for reasons stated* • *Identify specific actions planned or programmed to redress any shortfalls*	**Activity IV, Plan Review** • *Review the supported combatant command's OPLAN for legal sufficiency and make appropriate recommendations* • *Coordinate legal issues with counterparts*
Activity V, Supporting Plans • *Resolve critical issues that arise during the supported combatant command's review of supporting plan*	**Activity V, Supporting Plans** • *Crosswalk supporting plans to ensure that they are legally correct, complete, and consistent, and make appropriate recommendations*

Figure II-4. Adaptive Planning and Execution System Deliberate Planning Duties and Responsibilities

of CAP. As the planning process moves into the CAP execution phase, legal advisors of supporting and component organizations provide operational planning support.

ADAPTIVE PLANNING AND EXECUTION SYSTEM CRISIS ACTION PLANNING DUTIES AND RESPONSIBILITIES

Secretary of Defense	General Counsel of the Department of Defense
• *Approve alert orders* • *Approve deployment orders* • *Approve operation orders* • *Approve execute orders* • *Approve rules of engagement (ROE) and rules for the use of force (RUF) requests*	• *Ensure that all plans, orders, policies, ROE, and RUF, and target lists are reviewed for compliance with applicable law and policy as required by Department of Defense Directive (DODD) 2311.01E, DOD Law of War Program* • *Provide overall legal guidance related to prompt reporting, investigation and appropriate action under the DOD Law of War Program for alleged violations of the law of war* • *Coordinate DOD-wide legal support* • *Coordinate legal issues with interagency lawyer's working group as appropriate*
Chairman of the Joint Chiefs of Staff	**Legal Counsel**
Component I, Situation Awareness • *Situation Development. Detect, report, and assess events that have potential national security implications to determine whether a military response may be required.* • *Crisis Assessment. Analyze the situation and advise the President and/or Secretary of Defense (SecDef) of possible military action. Obtain a decision by the President and/or SecDef to develop military options.*	*Component I, Situation Awareness* • *Situation Development* • *Review planning documents* • *Contact counterparts and establish the basis for concurrent planning* • *Review applicable laws, policies, treaties, and agreements* • *Summarize relevant legal considerations (authorities, restraints, and constraints) and provide them to the Joint Staff, CJCS, and counterparts* • *Crisis Assessment. Refine the legal considerations, authorities, and constraints.* • *Participate in boards, cells and working groups as required*
Component II, Planning • *Course of Action (COA) Development. Issue planning guidance directive, normally in the form of a Chairman of the Joint Chiefs of Staff (CJCS) warning or planning order.* • *Detailed Plan Development. Detailed planning begins with the CJCS-issue planning or alert order. CJCS monitors the execution planning activities and reviews the supported commander's operation order or execute order for adequacy and feasibility.*	*Component II, Planning* • *Incorporate legal considerations and instructions for developing ROE/RUF in the combatant commander's planning guidance* • *Review the supported combatant commander's estimate for compliance with law and policy and make appropriate recommendations* • *Coordinate legal issues with counterparts*
Component III, Execution • *CJCS publishes the execute order following approval by SecDef* • *CJCS monitors the deployment and employment of forces and takes action as needed*	*Component III, Execution* • *Monitor operations for legal issues as required*

Figure II-5. Adaptive Planning and Execution System Crisis Action Planning Duties and Responsibilities

ADAPTIVE PLANNING AND EXECUTION SYSTEM CRISIS ACTION PLANNING DUTIES AND RESPONSIBILITIES (cont'd)

Combatant Commanders	Staff Judge Advocate
Component I, Situation Awareness	**Component I, Situation Awareness**
● *Situation Development. Detect, report, and assess events that have potential national security implications to determine whether a military response may be required.* ● *Crisis Assessment. Report actions being taken, forces available, expected time for earliest commitment of forces, and major constraints on the employment of forces. Keep the President and/or SecDef and CJCS informed of new developments. Establish a newsgroup supporting the crisis action, and announce it by message.*	● *Situation Development* ● *Contact legal counterparts and establish the basis for concurrent planning* ● *Review planning documents* ● *Review applicable laws, policies, treaties, agreements, and arrangements in all affected areas of responsibility (AORs)* ● *Summarize relevant legal considerations (authorities, restraints, and constraints) and provide them to the crisis action team, combatant commanders, and counterparts* ● *Crisis Assessment. Refine the legal considerations.*
Component II, Planning	**Component II, Planning**
● *COA Development* ● *In coordination with subordinate and supporting commanders, develop and analyze COAs* ● *Review and use applicable plans* ● *Detailed Plan Development* ● *Issue guidance to subordinate and supporting commanders for time-phased force and deployment data development* ● *Submit the commander's estimate to the President and/or SecDef and CJCS* ● *Begin detailed execution planning upon receipt of a planning order or alert order*	● *Incorporate legal considerations and instructions for developing ROE and RUF in the combatant commander's planning guidance* ● *Review the combatant commander's estimate for compliance with law and policy and make appropriate recommendations* ● *Coordinate legal issues and support requirements with counterparts* ● *Contact legal counterparts and facilitate concurrent planning* ● *Review and validate any judge advocate joint task force joint manning document requirements and synchronize joint legal support* ● *Participate in boards, cells and working groups, as required*
Component III, Execution	**Component III, Execution**
● *Execute the operation order* ● *Report force shortfalls to CJCS for resolution*	● *Monitor operations for legal issues as required* ● *Ensure legal arrangements for deployment/redeployment with host nations are in place through US embassies on all affected AORs*

Figure II-5. Adaptive Planning and Execution System Crisis Action Planning Duties and Responsibilities (cont'd)

For detailed guidance on APEX, see Chairman of the Joint Chiefs of Staff Manual (CJCSM) 3122.01A, Joint Operation Planning and Execution System Vol I: (Planning Policies, and Procedures); *CJCSM 3122.02C,* Joint Operation Planning and Execution System Vol III: (Crisis Action Time-Phased Force and Deployment Data Development and Deployment Execution, *CJCSM 3122.03C,* Joint Operation Planning and Execution System Vol II: Planning Formats; *Chairman of the Joint Chiefs of Staff Instruction*

(CJCSI) 3100.01A, Joint Strategic Planning System; *and the* User's Guide for Joint Operation Planning and Execution System.

4. Legal Support to Operational Level Planning

a. At the operational level, the supported CCDR may retain planning responsibility or delegate planning responsibility to a subordinate JFC, typically the commander of a JTF or a Service component commander. Regardless of the level of command, the legal advisor has a key support role in developing legally sufficient plans and orders that support achievement of the operational objectives.

MILITARY LAWYERS IN IRAQ

Military lawyers were true combat multipliers in Iraq. They were not only invaluable in dealing with a host of operational law issues, they also made enormous contributions in helping resolve a host of issues that were more than a bit out of normal legal lanes. In essence, we "threw" lawyers at very difficult problems and they produced solutions in virtually every case – often under very challenging circumstances and in an uncertain security environment. The qualities that make a great military lawyer – an individual who is smart, hard-working, logical in thought, a good writer, and an adjudicator – were precisely the qualities most in demand in the environment in which we found ourselves in Iraq, where we were both fighting and rebuilding. I tried to get all the lawyers we could get our hands on – and then sought more.

**SOURCE: Major General David H. Petraeus, Commander
101st Airborne Division (Air Assault) 2003-2004**

---

b. During the joint operation planning process, the joint force SJA prepares the legal estimate, plans legal support for the joint force, and contributes to the overall planning effort in accordance with the planning considerations detailed below.

(1) General Planning Considerations

(a) Throughout the operational planning process, the joint force SJA prepares the legal estimate and provides the commander, staff and appropriate planning boards, centers, and cells with advice and recommendations regarding legal issues that impact the full spectrum of the operation. The SJA reviews and monitors relevant legal aspects of potential COAs and evaluates the potential legal consequences resulting from primary and secondary effects. The SJA must also consider the law of war principles of military necessity, unnecessary suffering, distinction, and proportionality during planning.

(b) The joint force SJA should be familiar with the unique capabilities of component legal organizations and understand their role in supporting the JFC's concept of operations. The joint force SJA's ultimate goal includes promoting effectiveness, synchronizing unity of effort, and preventing unnecessary duplication of functions among component organizations. The joint force SJA's concept of support should address deployment, entry, buildup, application, identification and prioritization of areas of support, and redeployment of legal resources.

MISSION ANALYSIS

Staff Processes	Staff Judge Advocate's Actions

Staff Processes

- Determine known facts, current status, and conditions (including time analysis)
- Develop assumptions
- Analyze combatant commander's (CCDRs) mission and intent; determine limitations
- Develop enemy and own centers of gravity and decisive points
- Identify tasks (specified and implied)
- Analyze initial force structure requirements
- Assess risks
- Determine the military end state
- Develop the mission statement
- Present mission analysis brief

Staff Judge Advocate's Actions

- Participates in the core planning cell of the joint planning group (JPG)
- Identify legal support requirements
- Contact legal counterparts at higher, lower, and adjacent headquarters at the earliest opportunity and establish the basis for concurrent planning
- Review all planning documents
- Assist the CCDR by advising of legal issues relating to known facts, current status, and/or conditions. Determine own specified, implied, and essential tasks. Assist the commander by identifying legal issues impacting operational limitations. Provide guidance as to legal issues that have the potential to impact own military end state, objectives, and initial effects, as well as those that may impact initial commander's critical information requirements. Review strategic communication guidance, when applicable, for legal issues. Assist in the conduct of initial force structure analysis and initial risk assessment, highlighting any areas of legal concern. Assist with the development of the mission statement to ensure no legal objections. Assist with initial staff estimates to ensure no legal objections. Review commander's planning guidance and initial intent to confirm no legal objections/issues.
- Research applicable domestic, international, and foreign laws, policies, treaties, and agreements
- Summarize relevant legal considerations (authorities, restraints, and constraints) and provide them to the JPG
- Consider assigned mission, current situation, next higher commander's intent, United Nations Security Council resolutions, Standing Rules of Engagement (ROE)/Rules for the Use of Force (RUF), approved supplemental ROE/RUF, multinational ROE/RUF, and fiscal constraints

Figure II-6. Mission Analysis

(2) **Mission Analysis** (see Figure II-6). The joint planning staff's focus in operational planning begins with mission analysis. **The SJA (or a SJA representative) is a member of the core planning cell as soon as planning begins.** The joint force SJA's primary responsibility is to identify legal considerations (authorities, restraints, and constraints) and provide them to the commander and other planners to shape the initial planning guidance. Failure to identify legal considerations early in the planning process may waste precious time as the staff develops COAs that may not be legally feasible.

(3) **COA Development** (see Figure II-7).

(a) During COA development, COAs are proposed and evaluated to ensure that they are adequate, feasible, acceptable, distinguishable, and complete. In addition to the strict application of law, operational law issues frequently involve the implementation and interpretation of policy. To provide counsel on operational law

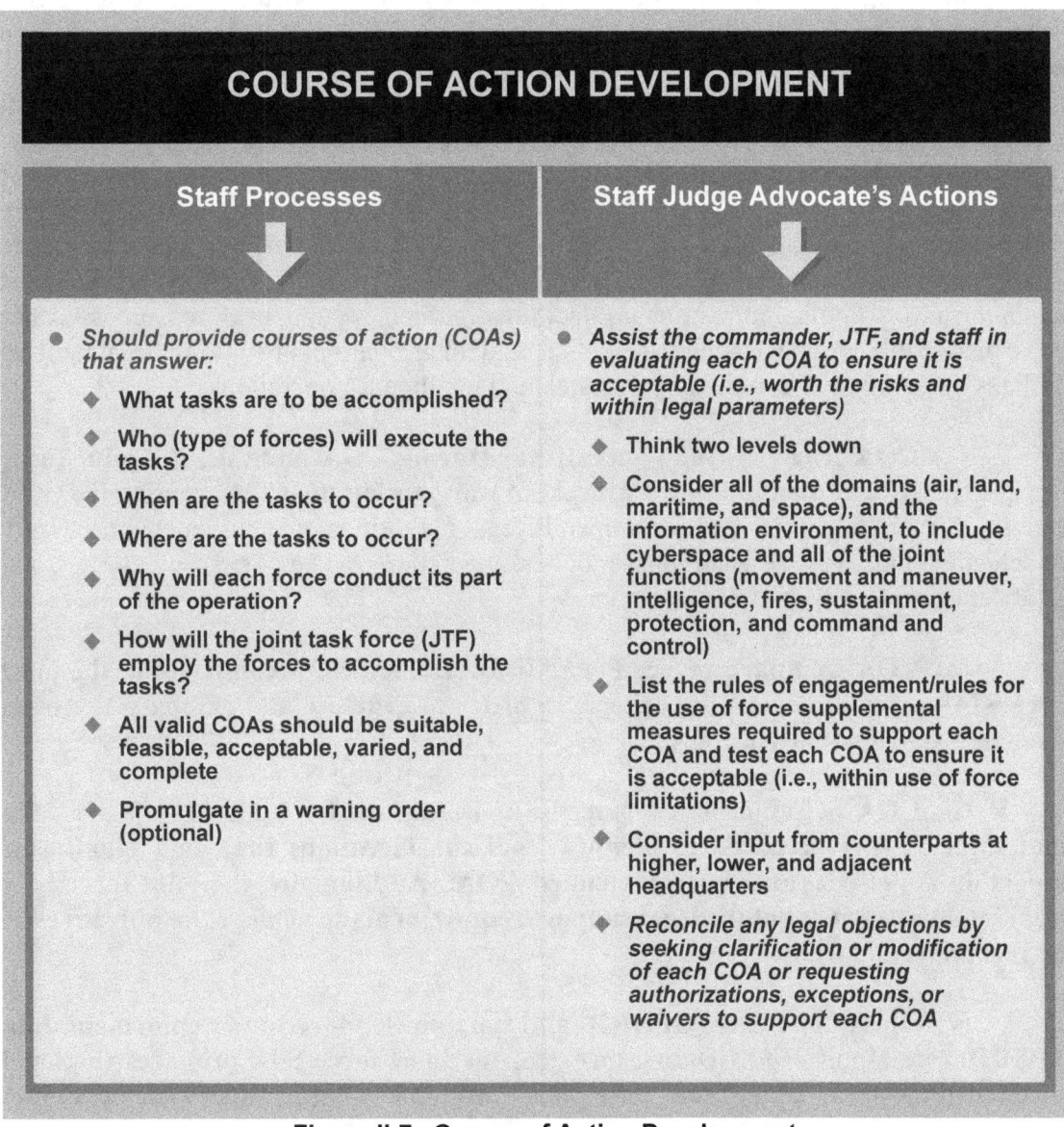

COURSE OF ACTION DEVELOPMENT

Staff Processes	**Staff Judge Advocate's Actions**
• *Should provide courses of action (COAs) that answer:*	• *Assist the commander, JTF, and staff in evaluating each COA to ensure it is acceptable (i.e., worth the risks and within legal parameters)*
◆ What tasks are to be accomplished?	
◆ Who (type of forces) will execute the tasks?	◆ Think two levels down
◆ When are the tasks to occur?	◆ Consider all of the domains (air, land, maritime, and space), and the information environment, to include cyberspace and all of the joint functions (movement and maneuver, intelligence, fires, sustainment, protection, and command and control)
◆ Where are the tasks to occur?	
◆ Why will each force conduct its part of the operation?	
◆ How will the joint task force (JTF) employ the forces to accomplish the tasks?	
◆ All valid COAs should be suitable, feasible, acceptable, varied, and complete	◆ List the rules of engagement/rules for the use of force supplemental measures required to support each COA and test each COA to ensure it is acceptable (i.e., within use of force limitations)
◆ Promulgate in a warning order (optional)	◆ Consider input from counterparts at higher, lower, and adjacent headquarters
	◆ *Reconcile any legal objections by seeking clarification or modification of each COA or requesting authorizations, exceptions, or waivers to support each COA*

Figure II-7. Course of Action Development

issues, the SJA must be able to spot the issue, and make appropriate recommendations. The SJA must consider the second and third order effects of each recommendation and provide a risk assessment of each COA. This requires keeping abreast of current events from the local, national, and international levels. The SJA reviews the COA's compliance with the law and policy. **If a COA is legally objectionable, the joint force SJA should seek clarification or amendment of the COA, or recommend that the JFC request appropriate authorizations, exceptions, or waivers.**

(b) The joint force SJA reviews other staff section proposals for legal sufficiency. As an example, the joint force SJA assists other staff elements (typically the operations directorate of a joint staff [J-3] or the plans directorate of a joint staff [J-5]), in determining **whether the standing rules of engagement/standing rules for the use of force are sufficient** to accomplish the mission, and, if not, **which supplemental ROE/RUF measures are needed and why.** The joint force SJA should consider and assist other staff elements in considering, for example, whether and under what circumstances the JFC should request or authorize the following: authority to declare forces as hostile (who and under what circumstances); use of riot control agents; offensive operations; cross border operations; use of all necessary means during special operations; collective self-defense (defense of non-US persons and property); beyond visual range engagement of airborne objects; exercise of national self-defense; use of wartime reserve modes; training or spotlighting with a directed energy weapon; adjustments to acceptable levels of collateral damage (LOAC-standard); engaging space assets; computer network operations; and operations affecting designated lines of communications, civilian infrastructure, facilities, and major supplies or resources. Other areas that require review include detention and interrogation operations, treatment of civilians, integration of contractor personnel, and intelligence operations.

(4) **COA Analysis** (see Figure II-8). **During COA analysis, the joint force SJA participates in the disciplined process of war gaming the COA.** During the COA analysis, the SJA identifies and recommends legal authorities or requirements necessary to achieve objectives at each phase of the operation. The legal advantages and disadvantages of each COA are identified.

(5) **COA Comparison** (see Figure II-8). **During COA comparison, the joint force SJA assists in developing criteria in order to evaluate and compare the legal issues associated with each COA.**

(6) **COA Selection** (see Figure II-8). During the COA brief to the JFC, **the joint force SJA is prepared to identify legal considerations that have significant impact on any aspect of the recommended COA. Additionally, the joint force SJA provides an assessment of the legal support requirements to achieve the objectives of the recommended COA.**

(7) **Operation order (OPORD) and time-phased force and deployment data (TPFDD)** (see Figure II-9). During this step, **the joint force SJA prepares the legal considerations paragraph of the "base plan" and the legal appendix to the personnel**

COURSE OF ACTION ANALYSIS (WAR GAMING) / COMPARISON / SELECTION

Staff Processes

- *Serves to amplify the initial courses of action (COAs), show strengths and weaknesses, and further identify elements of execution of the COAs*
- *The threat's most likely and most dangerous COAs should be used to war game the friendly COAs*
- *Wargame the actions of the joint task force (JTF) two command levels down for increased fidelity*
- *Should help to synchronize JTF component actions*

COA COMPARISON

- *Determine comparison criteria*
- *Compare each friendly COA with enemy COAs in accordance with the comparison criteria*
- *Determine optimal COA that achieves desired operational objectives*

COA SELECTION

- *Brief recommended COA to the commander, JTF*

Staff Judge Advocate's Actions

- *Continue to refine legal considerations*
- *Wargame legal consequences of friendly actions, threat reactions, and friendly counteractions*
- *Review legal authorities throughout wargaming*
- *Determine whether any friendly actions or counteractions require approval by higher authority*

COA COMPARISON

- *Evaluate COAs in light of established criteria*
- *Provide additional comparison criteria*

COA SELECTION

- *Brief the legal considerations and assist other staff sections in briefing legal issues related to their planning (e.g., rules of engagement, detainees)*
- *Determine legal support requirements*

Figure II-8. Course of Action Analysis (War Gaming)/Comparison/Selection

annex. The joint force SJA also assists other planning staff sections with appendices that have significant legal components related to the operation, e.g., assisting the J-3 or J-5 in preparing the ROE appendix to the operations annex and the appendix on enemy prisoners of war (EPWs) and detainees. These should be prepared in accordance with CJCSM 3122.03C, *Joint Operation Planning and Execution System Vol II: Planning Formats*. In addition, the SJA assists the J-3 or J-5 in preparing ROE request and authorization messages in accordance with CJCSI 3121.01B, *Standing Rules of Engagement/Standing Rules for the Use of Force for US Forces*.

(a) The **legal considerations** paragraph of the OPORD contains a summary of any legal considerations that may affect implementation of the plan or order (e.g., status of forces, ROE, international agreements, law of war, and United Nations Security Council resolutions).

(b) The **legal appendix** to the personnel annex (always appendix 4 (Legal) to annex E (Personnel)) reflects the legal estimate developed during the planning process

---

PREPARE OPERATION ORDER AND TIME-PHASED FORCE AND DEPLOYMENT DATA / ISSUE SYNCHRONIZED OPERATION ORDER

Staff Processes	Staff Judge Advocate's Actions
• *Determine who is responsible for the "base plan" and the various annexes of the operation order (OPORD)*	• *Prepare the legal considerations paragraph of the "base plan" according to Chairman of the Joint Chiefs of Staff Manual (CJCSM) 3122.03C*
• *Write OPORD*	• *Prepare the legal appendix according to CJCSM 3122.03C*
• *Develop the time-phased force and deployment data*	• *Assist the J-3 (Operations)/J-5 (Plans) in preparing the rules of engagement (ROE) or rules for the use of force (RUF) appendix*
• *Brief/obtain approval for the final draft OPORD*	
• *Brief OPORD to components/other staff*	• *Assist the J-3/J-5 in preparing supplemental ROE or RUF request and authorization messages according to the format in Chairman of the Joint Chiefs of Staff Instruction 3121.01C, Standing Rules of Engagement/Standing Rules for the Use of Force for US Forces*
• *Publish/transmit final draft OPORD. Obtain component supporting plans.*	
• *Conduct crosswalks and backbriefs as directed*	
• *Modify OPORD as necessary and publish/transmit*	• *Monitor dissemination, training, and interpretation of ROE or RUF. Review all training tools used at lower echelons.*
	• *Review and crosswalk the combatant commander's, joint task force's, and components' OPORDs and any ROE or RUF authorization messages to ensure they are legally correct, complete, and consistent*
	• *Recommend fragmentary order(s) and changes to the ROE or RUF to correct any errors or omissions*

Figure II-9. Prepare Operation Order and Time-Phased Force and Deployment Data/Issue Synchronized Operation Order

and outlines the plan for legal support. The joint force SJA uses the legal appendix to describe the legal considerations in detail; cite applicable references, including inter-Service, host nation (HN), and reciprocal support agreements; define key terms; establish coordinating and other administrative instructions; and state policies and procedures for all legal matters within the joint operations area.

(c) The joint force SJA assists other staff sections in the preparation of annexes that have significant legal implications for the operation. Review of the entire OPORD is critical, but often the most significant legal issues are found in the appendices for operations including **ROE, EPWs and detainees, intelligence, logistics (specifically the contracting support plan), and force protection. The significance of each appendix will vary depending on the desired effects and objectives for each**

---

operation. The joint force SJA must read the entire OPORD to ensure it is consistent with applicable law and policy.

(d) In developing these planning products, the **joint force SJA continuously communicates with** and **solicits input from counterparts.** The Services and Service components retain responsibility for legal support to their forces, subject to the coordinating guidance of the joint force SJA issued under the authority of the JFC. When coordinating inter-Service legal support, the joint force SJA should consider ways to leverage limited resources (e.g., personnel, communications systems, and transportation) and avoid duplication of effort by recommending the JFC establish joint legal organizations or collocating single-Service legal organizations throughout the joint operations area (JOA), as appropriate. For multinational operations, close coordination with multinational force legal advisors is critical.

(8) **Issue and Synchronize OPORD** (see Figure II-9). During this step, the joint force **SJA reviews the higher, lower, and adjacent commanders' OPORDs to ensure synchronization, unity of effort, legal accuracy, completeness, and consistency.** The joint force SJA should attempt to correct any errors or omissions before the OPORDs are formally published.

(9) **Rehearsal.** The **joint force SJA attends the operations order rehearsal.** This is the joint force SJA's first opportunity to assess each commander's understanding of the applicable legal restraints and constraints on the operation. If there are inconsistencies, the joint SJA seeks clarification and amendment consistent with the legal restraints/constraints, or seeks authorizations, waivers, or exceptions to support the proposed actions. During the rehearsal, the SJA provides to the commander and staff any legal briefings and training pertinent to the operation (e.g., country law briefs and ROE or RUF situational training).

For detailed guidance on joint operation planning, see JP 5-0, Joint Operation Planning.

Intentionally Blank

CHAPTER III
LEGAL SUPPORT TO THE JOINT TASK FORCE

"Operational Law is going to become as significant to the commander as maneuver, as fire support, and as logistics. It will be a principal battlefield activity. The senior staff judge advocates may be as close to the commander as his operations officer or his chief of staff. They will be the right hand of the commander, and he will come to them for advice."

Lieutenant General Anthony C. Zinni
Commanding General, I Marine Expeditionary Force (1994-1996)

1. Introduction

a. As the principal legal advisor to the CJTF and JTF staff, the JTF SJA is responsible for the organization and employment of legal personnel assigned or attached to the JTF HQ. The JTF SJA provides full spectrum legal service to the JTF HQ and coordinates with the supported CCDR's SJA and supporting component SJAs to optimize legal support throughout the JTF.

b. This chapter provides guidance on establishing, staffing, training, equipping, and employing a JTF SJA section. Although this chapter focuses specifically on a JTF, it is an applicable framework for examining the key planning considerations of a joint force SJA at all echelons of command. This chapter describes the role, responsibilities, and key considerations of the JTF SJA throughout the JTF "life cycle" of forming, planning, deploying, employing, transitioning, and redeploying (see Figure III-1). Although this JTF "lifecycle" appears sequential and linear in progression, in reality, the JTF is a dynamic organization that typically operates in a time-sensitive and ever-changing environment that requires many actions to occur concurrently (see Figure III-2). The SJA section supporting a JTF HQ similarly must be dynamic in its organization, planning, training, and execution.

For additional information on forming a JTF HQ, see JP 3-33, Joint Task Force Headquarters.

2. Legal Support in the Joint Task Force Battle Rhythm

a. Each JTF develops a battle rhythm of daily events, briefings, and meetings that optimizes the information flow across the staff, allowing the organization to plan and execute the mission most effectively. The battle rhythm is a primary factor that drives the legal support requirements for the JTF HQ, including support to the boards, centers, cells, and working groups that plan and execute the JTF mission. It is through the battle rhythm that the JTF SJA identifies and responds to many of the legal support requirements of the JTF HQ and subordinate commands. An effective JTF SJA understands the JTF battle rhythm, as well as the collaborative information environment (CIE), and actively provides legal advice and counsel to the boards, centers, cells, and working groups of the JTF.

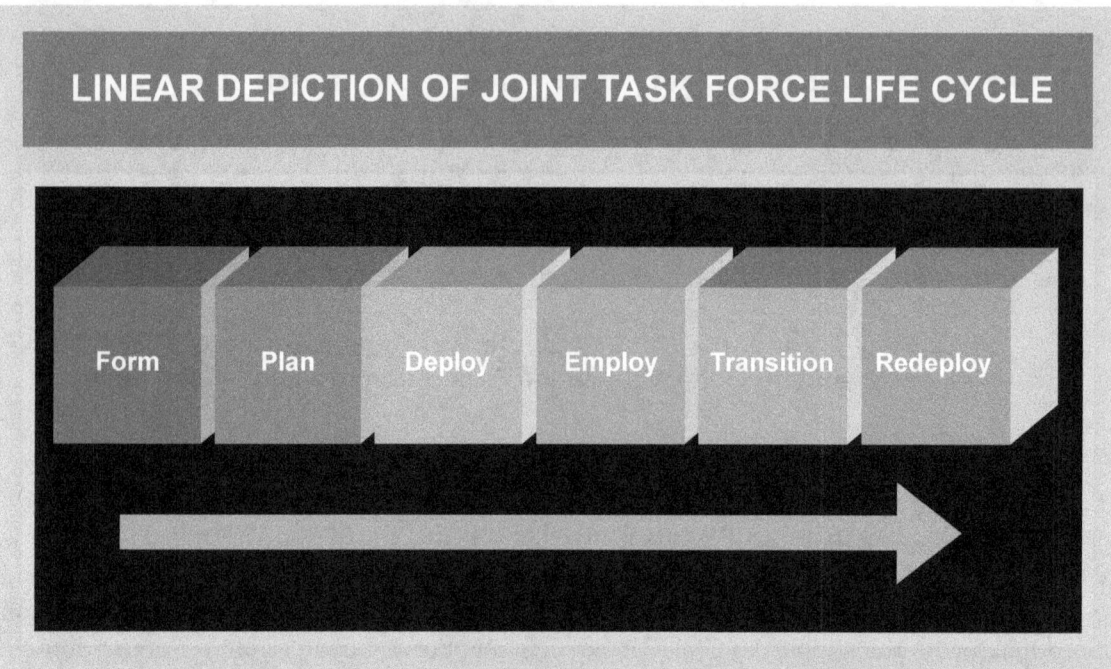

Figure III-1. Linear Depiction of Joint Task Force Life Cycle

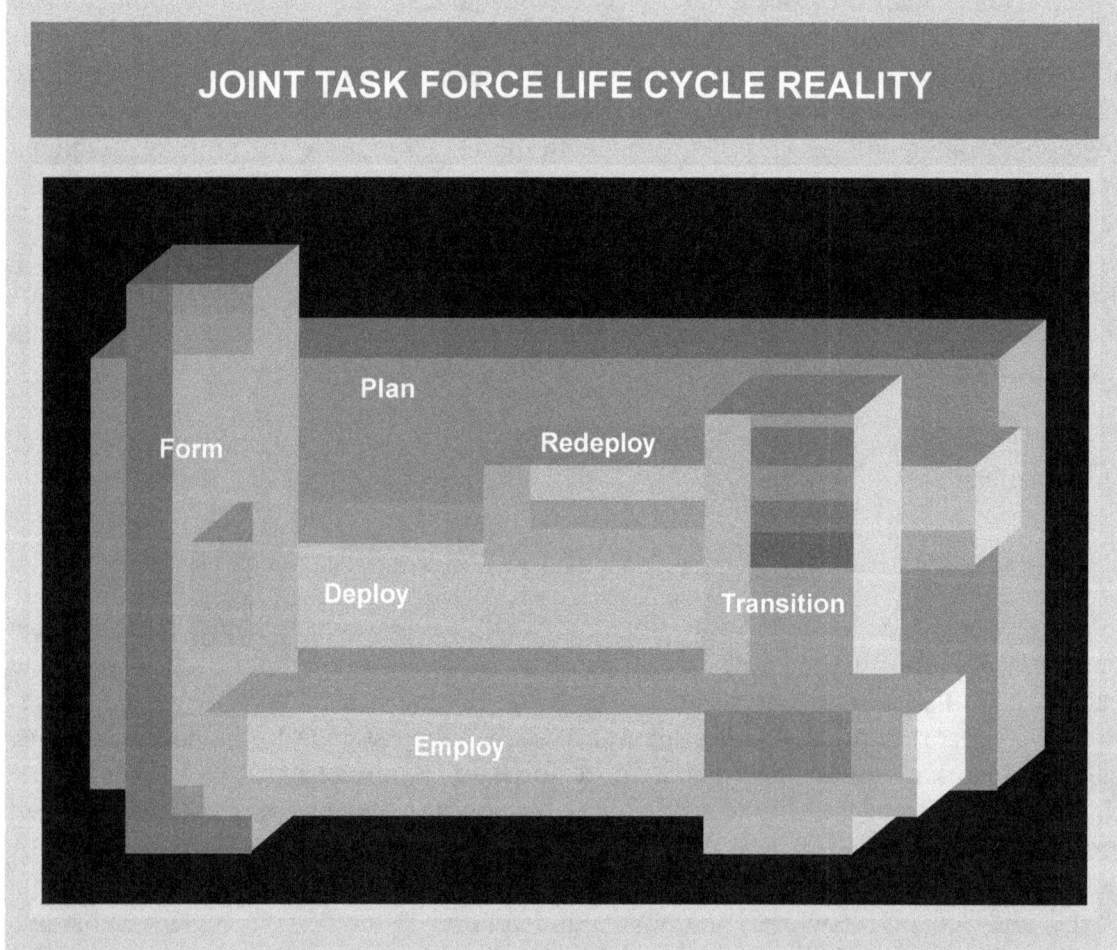

Figure III-2. Joint Task Force Life Cycle Reality

b. **Boards, Centers, Cells, and Working Groups**

(1) JTF mission planning and execution is conducted through various boards, centers, cells, and working groups formed to allow cross-functional synchronization of effort in a specific area of interest (see Figure III-3). Although the specific boards, centers, cells, and working groups vary according to the JTF mission, all should have a central planning group or joint planning group (JPG). The JTF SJA (or SJA representative) normally serves as a key member of the JPG. The JPG provides initial assessment of a crisis situation, advises the JFC concerning the organization of the JTF, and conducts CAP. The SJA, as a JPG member, is familiar with the CAP process and the APEX system products. The JTF SJA assists the JPG by identifying legal issues that may affect operational planning. To help with immediate legal support to the JPG, the JTF SJA section initially may be augmented by a judge advocate from a combatant command standing joint force headquarters (SJFHQ), a joint legal support element (JLSE) or similar entity.

(2) In addition to the JPG, the JTF SJA typically is a key member of the ROE/RUF planning cell, the information operations cell, the joint operations center (JOC), the joint security coordination center, the civil-military operations center, joint targeting coordination board (JTCB), the joint interrogation and detention facility board, the joint military police agency, the joint acquisition board, and the joint reception center. Legal advisors are also assigned as members of any board, center, or cell that will likely face significant legal issues on a recurring basis, for example, Medical Resource Boards.

For further details regarding the composition of a JTF see, JP 3-33, Joint Task Force Headquarters, *and JP 3-57,* Civil-Military Operations.

c. **Functional Areas.** In addition to the direct support provided to the boards, centers, cells, and working groups, the JTF SJA is prepared, either directly or through the CIE, to provide legal support to the CJTF and the entire staff across the full spectrum of legal functional areas. The functional areas include, but are not limited to, the following:

(1) Administrative law, including investigations;

(2) Air and space law;

(3) Business, commercial, and financial law;

(4) Claims;

(5) Contract law;

(6) Criminal law;

(7) Domestic operations law;

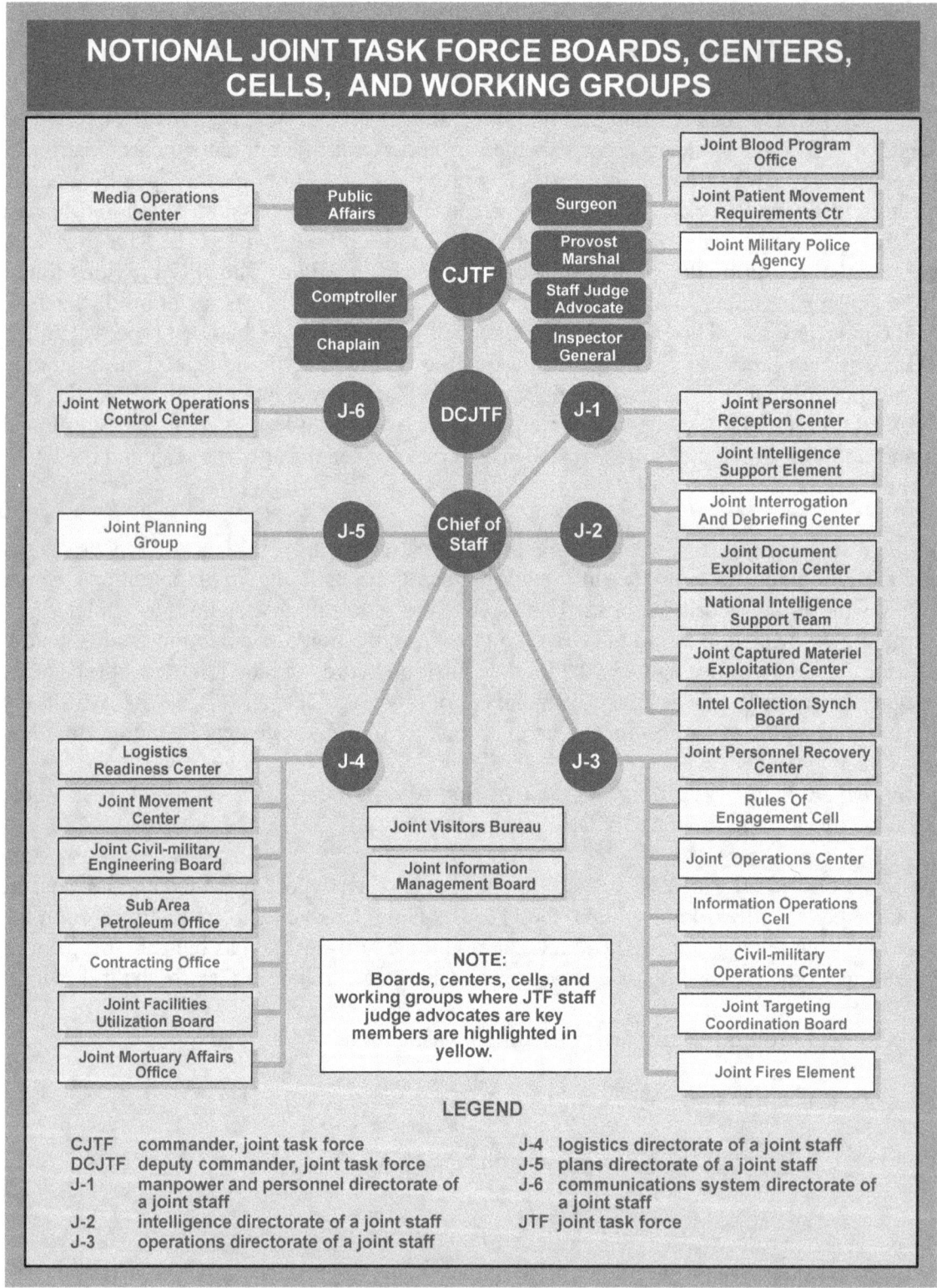

Figure III-3. Notional Joint Task Force Boards, Centers, Cells, and Working Groups

(8) Environmental law;

(9) Ethics and Standards of Conduct;

(10) Fiscal law;

(11) Intellectual property law;

(12) Intelligence law;

(13) International, comparative, and foreign law;

(14) Law of the sea;

(15) Law of war;

(16) Labor and civilian personnel law;

(17) Legal assistance;

(18) Legal training;

(19) Litigation;

(20) Medical law;

(21) Military Justice;

(22) Military personnel law, including adverse actions;

(23) Operational law;

(24) Real property law;

(25) Regulatory law;

(26) Tax law;

(27) Transportation law;

(28) Telecommunications law; and

(29) Laws and status of the RC.

For details regarding specific functional legal issues, see, Operational Law Handbook, The Judge Advocate General's Legal Center and School, *US Army* (2010); Air Force

Operations and the Law, *The Judge Advocate General's Corps, US Air Force (2d ed., 2009)*; *Judge Advocate General Instruction 5800.7E*, Manual of the Judge Advocate General, *Judge Advocate General's Corps, US Navy 2007*; *Navy Warfare Publication (NWP) 1-14M*, The Commander's Handbook on the Law of Naval Operations (2007).

3. Forming the Joint Task Force Staff Judge Advocate Section

a. Joint force SJAs at all levels are responsible for developing the organizational structure for their command SJA sections; but, unlike the JTF SJA, most are not required to form at the same time they are planning, training, and deploying for an operation. Because JTFs are established in a variety of different ways and for diverse missions, it is critically important for a JTF SJA to understand fully the legal support requirements of the particular JTF and how those requirements may change over time.

b. Designation as a JTF SJA often requires a transition from a single Service perspective to a broader joint operational view. JTF SJAs may initially be unfamiliar with the other service forces they will support as part of the JTF, but should be familiar with joint doctrine, processes, and procedure. Unlike Service component SJAs, who are responsible for their respective service legal organizations, the JTF SJA is responsible for integrating and synchronizing the wide range of legal capabilities available throughout the JTF. The JTF SJA must be familiar with the unique legal capabilities and limitations of the component forces and understand how best to employ them to support the CJTF's concept of operations. During the formation of the JTF SJA section, the JTF SJA must be in close coordination with counterparts at higher, lower, and adjacent headquarters to determine properly the optimal legal organization and staffing requirements.

c. The JTF SJA has many options for developing the organizational structure of the section. When determining the organization, staffing, and augmentation requirements, a JTF SJA should:

(1) Consider mission; enemy (forces and tactics); terrain and weather (operational environment); troops and support available (composition of the joint force); time available (for JTF forming and mission duration); civilian considerations (contractors, interagency personnel, nongovernmental and intergovernmental personnel, and international civilian organizations); language translation requirements; and political factors and the effect these factors will have on required legal support.

(2) Be prepared to operate according to the JTF staff's "battle rhythm" on a 24-hour cycle.

(3) Be prepared to support actively and provide SJA representation to the specific JTF boards, centers, cells, and working groups that require legal expertise in the planning and employment of JTF forces. This representation may require having a JA collocated with each board, center, or cell.

(4) Be prepared to provide appropriate functional area expertise and administrative support to the JTF HQ either directly or through reachback to functional experts via the CIE.

(5) Balance the SJA section staffing as to numbers, experience, influence of position, and rank of component, allied, and coalition members of the operation so as to provide the best possible legal advice and counsel to the JTF commander and staff.

(6) Reflect in the SJA section the composition of the joint force and character of the operation to ensure that the section understands the capabilities, legal requirements, and limitations of each component.

(7) Consider efficiencies of scale and Service component responsibilities.

(8) Define duties, roles, and relationships. Clearly defined duties, roles, and relationships are essential to forming a cohesive staff section and integrating and synchronizing the actions of the various legal organizations within the joint force SJA's area of concern.

(9) Understand the rotation policy for individual augmentees assigned to the joint force command. Although the CCDR ultimately establishes individual and unit rotation policies, the policies will not necessarily be uniform. To stabilize key billets, consider filling them with personnel with the longest tour lengths. However, this consideration must be balanced against the capabilities and talents of the individuals involved.

(10) Consider the level of familiarity that the section will have with regard to joint force doctrine and organizations.

(11) For multinational operations, conduct effective liaison with the legal staff of partner forces and coalition or allied headquarters legal staff.

(12) Understand the sourcing processes for augmenting the section or requesting specific legal capabilities.

(13) Become familiar with the administrative requirements of the various services, especially with regard to evaluations, mandatory counseling and fitness testing.

d. The organization, staffing, training, and equipping requirements of the JTF SJA section depends on many factors, but one constant is the need to build a task organized joint legal team. The JTF SJA's approach to jointness is the critical element in building this team. Important team-building tasks include defining responsibilities for direct and technical legal supervision and support.

4. Joint Task Force Staff Judge Advocate Manning

a. The SecDef and CCDRs have many options in establishing a JTF HQ. The JTF HQ can be established either by using a standing JTF HQ, by augmenting a core Service component HQ, or by forming an ad hoc HQ from multiple services. With any method, the CJTF will propose a JTF JMD that lists the personnel staffing requirements for all elements of that JTF HQ. The JTF SJA develops the personnel requirements for the SJA section and submits them to the manpower and personnel directorate for inclusion in the CJTF's proposed JMD. The development of the JTF SJA JMD is a critical step in ensuring optimal legal support for the JTF.

b. Historical reviews of past JTF JMDs and joint judge advocate working group evaluations of JTF SJA staffing requirements reveal that most JTF SJA sections require certain baseline staffing requirements to be capable of providing adequate legal support to the CJTF and staff. Although there is variability in staffing requirements for each JTF due to the factors listed above, a typical land-based JTF must be capable of operating on a 24-hour battle rhythm. This notional JTF SJA section, organized into three subsections—operational law, legal services, and administration—includes the following:

    (1) SJA;

    (2) Deputy SJA;

    (3) Chief, Operational Law;

    (4) Two to four Operational Law Attorneys (day and night operations);

    (5) One to two International Law Attorneys;

    (6) Chief, Legal Services;

    (7) One to two Contract/Fiscal Law Attorneys;

    (8) One to two Claims/Legal Assistance Law Attorneys;

    (9) Military Justice Practitioner;

    (10) One Legal Administrator; and

    (11) Four to six Paralegals.

c. The notional JTF SJA section reflects a starting point for SJA staff planning that ensures the many boards, centers, cells, and working groups of the JTF will receive effective legal support. As the JTF grows or shrinks in the complexity of the mission, scope, or battle rhythm, the demand for legal support may change correspondingly. JMD template tools are available through the CIE that can assist the CCDR and JTF SJAs in developing the requirements for the SJA section manning (see Figure III-4).

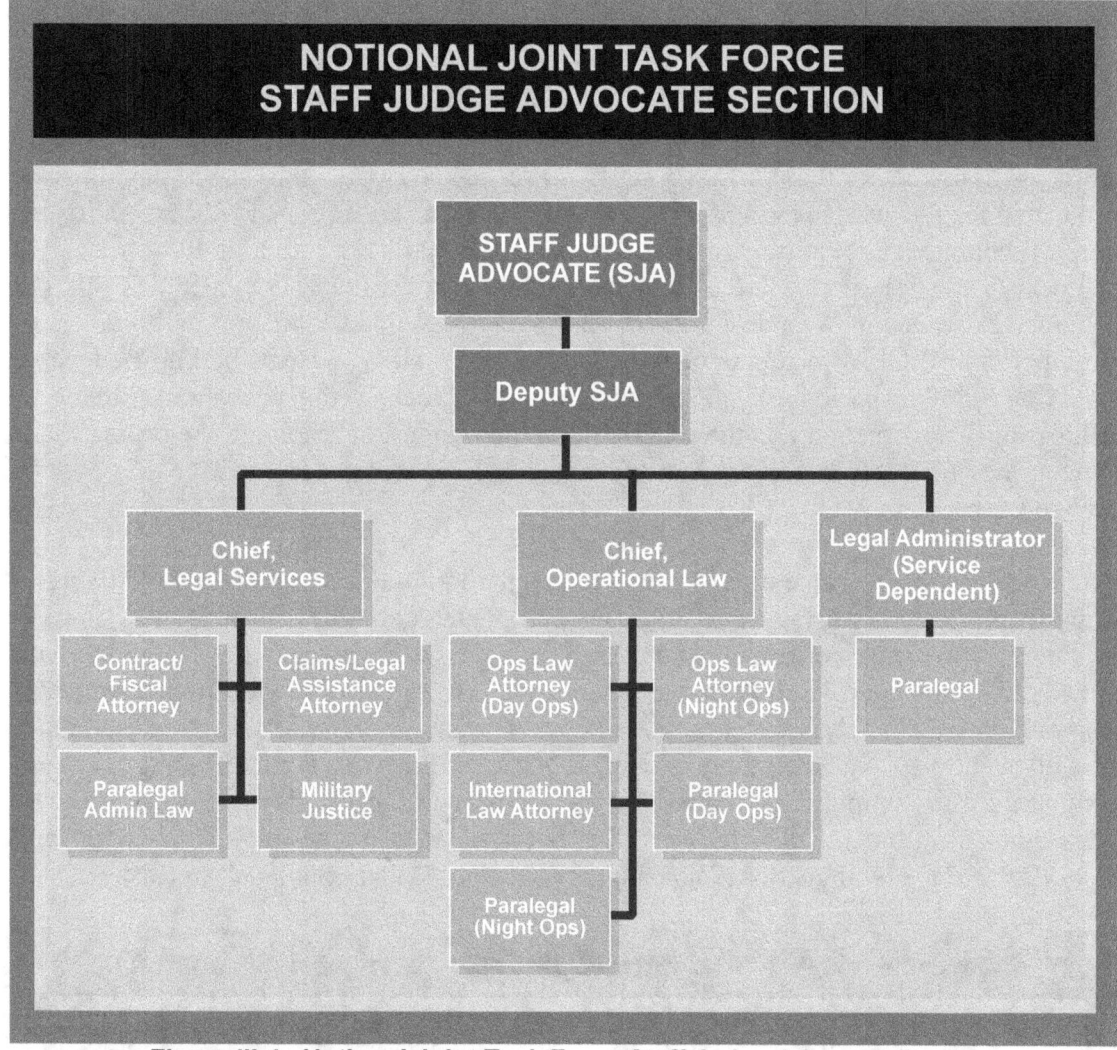

Figure III-4. Notional Joint Task Force Staff Judge Advocate Section

d. The supported CCDR SJA assists the CCDR in validating and sourcing personnel requirements for subordinate joint force SJA sections. The JTF SJA must maintain situational awareness while planning and controlling operations and be prepared to request modification of the JTF JMD as necessary. A resource for the JTF SJA is the Joint Judge Advocate Sourcing Working Group comprised of Service, supported combatant command, and USJFCOM SJA representatives who work to ensure that trained and qualified judge advocates and paralegals are sourced to fill specific JTF SJA JMD requirements.

e. **Augmentation of the SJA Section**

(1) The core JTF staff often is formed from an existing Service component HQ. This Service component HQ transforms into a joint organization and typically is augmented by other service or combat support agency personnel. For example, in a chemical, biological, radiological or nuclear incident, the SJA section can be augmented with functional legal capabilities from a DTRA consequence management advisory team

that is task organized to a CCDR's JTF during a crisis or incident. This augmentation may come in several forms. Immediate augmentation for CAP may come from part or all of the combatant command SJFHQ or from a JLSE, which is a multi-Service, multidisciplined legal enabling capability comprised of judge advocates or civilian attorneys assigned to the CCDR's staff. The SJFHQ JAs and JLSE can provide responsive legal expertise to the CJTF and staff during CAP. The SJFHQ JAs and JLSE do not function as a forward element of the CCDR's staff, but rather as fully integrated members of the JTF staff. These elements deploy to assist the JTF SJA in carrying out planning and execution responsibilities. The SJFHQ JAs and JLSE normally will have participated in CAP as members of the CCDR's battle staff and will be knowledgeable about the joint operation planning and execution process, the operational area, the political-military situation and the CCDR's plan and intent for resolving the crisis. If the SJFHQ does not include a judge advocate, the JTF SJA may ask the CCDR's SJA to provide a representative.

(2) Another source of SJA initial augmentation may come from a joint JA crisis action response cell (see Figure III-5). This cell, which could be sourced with JAs from combatant command components and/or Service HQs, provides the JTF SJA with immediate joint legal capability that augments the JTF SJA section until permanent JMD positions are adequately sourced and trained. A joint JA crisis action response cell is typically a short-term augmentation for an ad hoc JTF HQ. A JTF SJA needing this team could request the support as a request for forces through the JTF J-3. This cell, like the judge advocate from the SJFHQ or JLSE, becomes part of the JTF SJA section and provides the JTF SJA immediate legal support in critical functional legal specialties.

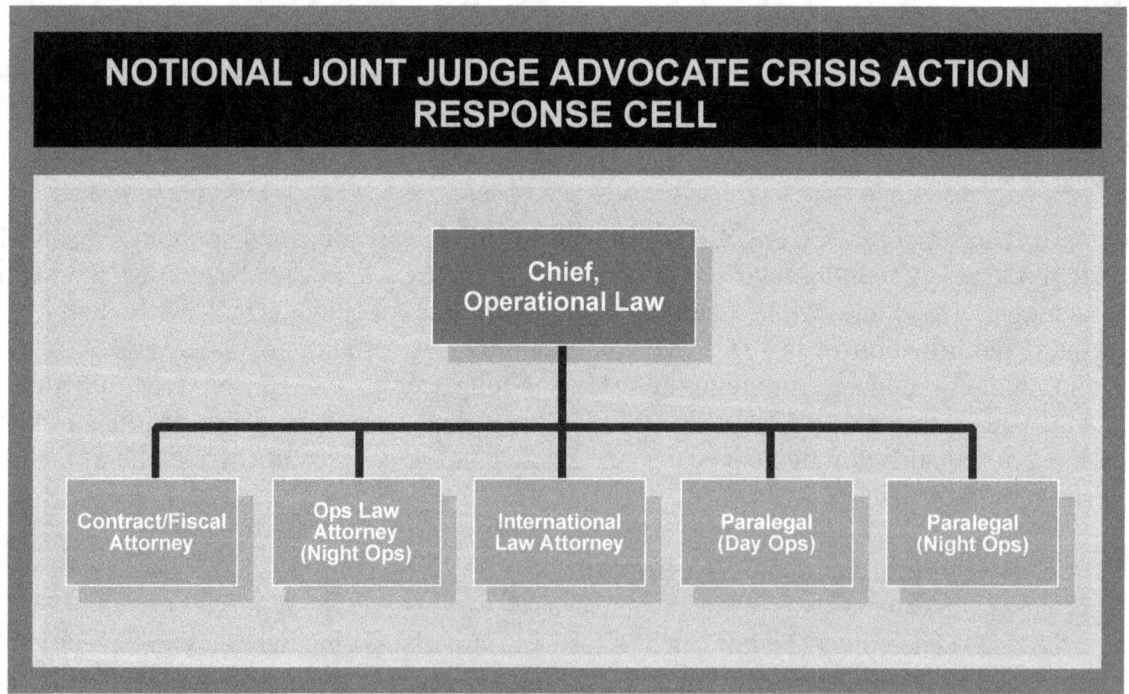

Figure III-5. Notional Joint Judge Advocate Crisis Action Response Cell

(3) The policy and procedures for obtaining individual augmentees (versus augmentation of a capability by a cell) for the JMD is prescribed in CJCSI 1301.01C, *Individual Augmentation Procedures*. Individual augmentees to the JTF are positions specifically listed on the JTF JMD and coordinated for sourcing through the manpower and personnel directorate of a joint staff (J-1). The CCDR assigns missions to subordinate JFCs and validates the forces required to accomplish those missions. Once validated, the CCDR secures the required augmentees from the combatant command staff and component commands. (Exception: Requirements for SOF are sourced directly through theater special operations commands to USSOCOM.) The combatant command components source as much of the required joint force as possible from internal resources. Remaining requirements are passed to the appropriate Service headquarters for individual augmentee sourcing.

(4) The Joint JA Sourcing Working Group comprised of Service, combatant command, and Joint Staff representatives, monitors and makes recommendations for sourcing of JAs for joint legal support requirements. The working group provides joint JA sourcing solutions for J-3 requests for forces and for J-1 individual augmentation. The working group makes recommendations to the prioritization sourcing review boards conducted for each JTF to ensure that the SJA sections of each JTF are adequately sourced from the appropriate service and with the appropriate legal and other necessary operational skill qualifications and training.

5. **Joint Staff Judge Advocate Training**

a. **Joint training**—the cornerstone to joint readiness—is one of the most critical components to providing adequate legal support to the JTF. There are two components of joint SJA training—individual and organizational.

b. **Individual Joint Training.** To ensure that the JTF SJA section can provide adequate legal support to the JTF, the SJA must ensure that assigned or attached personnel have the requisite individual training. All members of the JTF SJA section must have training in three areas – legal, joint, and tactical (see Figure III-6). Although the level of experience and/or training in joint operations and legal issues may vary based upon the position and rank, all personnel must have commensurate operational training.

(1) **Legal Training.** Each Service provides Service-specific operational law training that focuses on the primary activities of that service. This training provides the foundation for the legal expertise needed to advise the JTF in service specific areas of operation (e.g., air operations, space operations, maritime operations, and ground maneuver operations, regional language and cultural training, and host country law training) and meets the minimum legal training requirements to serve in a JTF SJA section. This training, however, may be inadequate for the JTF SJA or supervisors in the JTF SJA section (e.g., chief, operational law section and chief, legal services section) because it does not provide sufficiently broad overview of legal issues at the joint operational level. JTF SJA and supervisory JAs typically require advanced operational law instruction and/or significant prior operational law experience. Before serving as the

SKILLS SETS FOR THE JOINT TASK FORCE JUDGE ADVOCATE

Legal Skills	Joint Skills	Tactical Skills
Noncombatants	National Security Structure	Weapons Qualification
Post-Conflict Operations	Joint Staff Structure	CBRN
Civil-Military Operations	Task Organization/ Command & Support Relationships	Force Protection (Convoy Operations, IED recognition, etc.)
Humanitarian Assistance/Disaster Relief		First Aid
Rule of Law	Military Decision-Making Process	Communications
Peace Operations	Plans/Orders	Navigation
Irregular Warfare	APEX/Joint Planning	Troop Leading Procedures
Joint Military Justice	Targeting Operations	Military Briefing
	Staff Studies	JOC Watch Standing
	Leadership/Training	Licensed to Operate/Drive Tactical Vehicle (e.g., HMMWV
	JPME1	
	Foreign Disclosure/Security	

LEGEND

APEX	Adaptive Planning and Execution	IED	improvised explosive device
CBRN	chemical, biological, radiological, and nuclear	JOC	joint operations center
HMMWV	high mobility multipurpose wheeled vehicle	JPME1	joint professional military education (phase 1)

Figure III-6. Skills Sets for the Joint Task Force Judge Advocate

JTF SJA or a supervisory JA, senior JAs should attend the Joint Operational Law Course. This course provides advanced legal and joint training focused on the joint operational environment.

(2) **Joint Training.** The JTF SJA understands that joint doctrine is different from their Service doctrine and procedures. It is important that the JTF SJA section similarly understand the broad joint planning and employment processes and products. Accordingly, JAs assigned or attached to a JTF should be qualified as Joint Professional Military Education-1 by completing a qualifying course, either in residence or by correspondence.

(3) **Tactical Training.** All legal personnel supporting a JTF must be prepared to operate in a deployed joint environment that requires individual and unit force protection measures, including the ability to move tactically or coordinate movement

throughout the operational environment. Not all of these skills are usually required of JAs within the various Services. Consequently, certain operational skills must be acquired before embarking for service in a JTF SJA section. Operational skills training should include the following and may be augmented depending on mission requirements:

(a) Qualification with individually assigned weapon and familiarization on weapons personnel may be exposed to while traversing the battlefield, to include, but not limited to, the M-9, M-4/M16A2, M-249 SAW and MAG 240;

(b) Chemical, biological, radiological, and nuclear defense training;

(c) Force protection training;

(d) Land navigation training;

(e) JOC watch standing training (e.g., JOC procedures during troops in contact call, friendly fire incident);

(f) Communications training;

(g) Convoy operations training (including operation of various tactical vehicles and local traffic laws, route assessment, selection, order of movement, rest stops, improvised explosive device procedures, vehicle recovery procedures, medical evacuation [MEDEVAC] procedures, and enemy contact procedures [flee or pursue]);

(h) First aid training (combat lifesaver course or advanced medical training, if available, include 9-line MEDEVAC); and,

(i) Detainee handling procedures (e.g., search, evidence handling and chain of custody during transport).

(4) When a JAG or paralegal has completed all three areas of training, the respective Services should be able to track and identify those JAGs and paralegals to facilitate the timeliness of the augmentation sourcing process (see Figure III-7).

c. **Organizational JTF SJA Training.** The JTF SJAs organizational training responsibilities fall into two categories, SJA section training and CJTF and staff training.

(1) **SJA Section Training**

(a) The JTF SJA, like the rest of the JTF staff, is responsible for assisting the CJTF in developing the command's joint mission-essential task list and joint training plan (JTP), in executing the command's joint training and exercise program, and in assessing the command's mission capability and any strengths or deficiencies in doctrine, organization, training, materiel, or education. In addition, the JTF SJA is responsible for identifying supporting tasks performed by the SJA section and in assisting subordinate

COMPETENCIES FOR JOINT TASK FORCE STAFF JUDGE ADVOCATE SECTION MEMBERS

DUTY TITLE	TRAINING/EXPERIENCE
Staff Judge Advocate	*Operational Skills/JOLC/Significant OPLAW Experience and Related Joint HQ Experience, Reserve Components Matters*
Deputy Staff Judge Advocate	*Operational Skills/JOLC/Significant OPLAW Experience or Related Joint HQ Experience*
Chief, Legal Services Claims/Legal Assistance Attorney	*Operational Skills/JOLC/Contract and Fiscal Law Courses or Subject Matter Experience*
Contract/Fiscal Law Attorney	*Operational Skills/JOLC/Subject Matter Experience*
Chief, OPLAW	*Operational Skills/JOLC Operational Skills/JOLC/LLM in International/Military Law or Significant Subject Matter Experience*
OPLAW Attorneys	*Operational Skills/LOMO or OPLAW Course or JAGFLAG or Subject Matter Experience*
International Law Attorney	*Operational Skills/JOLC/LLM in International/Military Law or Subject Matter Experience*
Legal Administrator	*Operational Skills*
Operational Paralegals	*Operational Skills/CoC Familiarization*
Paralegals	*Operational Skills*

LEGEND

CoC	Code of Conduct	LLM	*Legum Magister* (Master of Laws)
HQ	headquarters	LOMO	Law of Military Operations course
JAGFLAG	Air Force operations law course	OPLAW	operational law
JOLC	joint operational law course		

Figure III-7. Competencies for Joint Task Force Staff Judge Advocate Section Members

component SJAs in identifying supporting tasks performed by their sections. The JTF SJA also is responsible for developing a supporting SJA JTP to prepare the SJA section for its mission. The JTF SJA's JTP should supplement rather than duplicate the command's JTP.

For further detail on the development of the JTP, see CJCSM 3500.03B, Joint Training Manual for the Armed Forces of the United States.

(b) Successful legal support to the JTF depends on a well-integrated legal team where each member of the section understands the overall JTF mission, the operations of the JTF, the responsibilities of the JTF SJA section, and their specific role within the organization. Because the JTF is augmented with personnel from different services and from Active and Reserve Components, the JTF section training program should include an orientation to the specific JTF HQ that includes the boards, centers, and cells that the SJA directly supports, the JTF SJA section organization scheme, and computer training to ensure that all JTF JAs can utilize the CIE effectively. Depending on the JTF mission and environment, the section may also require training on section movement procedures including office breakdown and set-up, convoy procedures, and force protection measures.

(c) In preparation for mission execution and time permitting, the fully augmented JTF SJA section should participate in a mission rehearsal exercise along with the entire JTF. This joint exercise assists the JTF SJA section in refining office procedure and JOC watch standing, improving JTF staff coordination and integration, and identifies potential shortfalls in manning, training, and equipping of the section before actual deployment.

(2) **JTF Command and Staff Training.** The JFC and the JTF HQ staff will require training on the legal aspects of the JTF mission. The SJA typically provides training on the following:

(a) LOAC;

(b) ROE/RUF;

(c) Host country or applicable domestic law;

(d) Detention operations, including point of capture procedures

1. Evidence collection and exploitation;

2. Interrogation;

3. Detention center operations;

4. Adjudication by tribunal, commission, or other system of justice;

(e) Ethics and Standards of Conduct;

(f) Procurement/fiscal considerations and constraints;

(g) Claims process;

(h) Other legal issues identified in the mission analysis.

6. **Equipping the Joint Task Force Staff Judge Advocate**

a. A key component of the legal support to the JTF is the development of the equipment and logistics requirements for the JTF SJA section. Although Service component SJA offices often have organic equipment to perform their Service-specific legal support, a JTF SJA section typically will not have the organic equipment that is necessary to perform the entire joint legal support mission. The same factors that drive the manning requirements will affect the JTF SJA determination of the section's equipment and logistics requirements. The mission, environment, composition of the joint force, size of the SJA section, JTF battle rhythm, and location of the section personnel supporting the boards, centers, and cells, are key factors affecting the equipment requirements. The individual, the section, the law library and other research capabilities, and the necessity for SJA section participation in the CIE should be considered to help determine equipment requirements. Considering these factors, the equipment development process should:

(1) Identify equipment and facilities requirements relative to each JTF billet.

(2) Identify communications system requirements (e.g., video teleconferencing, such as E-Collab or Defense Connect Online) with the CCDR's SJA and component SJAs; internet access for legal research; local area network and telephone; digital sender, digital camera, and tactical satellite communications capability; computer requirements (laptops versus desktops); and printers. Consider whether operations require secure communications.

(3) Identify transportation requirements (vehicles, containers and qualified drivers) for all JTF SJA personnel and equipment. Consider timelines for container movement.

(4) Identify equipment (particularly computer hardware and software) necessary to participate in the CIE (e.g., information workspace software) and conduct reach-back to sources of technical legal expertise such as the International and Operational Law Divisions of the Service Judge Advocates General and the Army's Center for Law and Military Operations.

(5) Assess legal library requirements given the environment and the force composition.

(6) Identify field office requirements, including tentage, field desks, power generators, etc.

(7) Identify access, password, and clearance requirements that allow JTF SJA personnel access to necessary computer-based legal references and resources. For example, security clearances that allow access to the SECRET Internet Protocol Router Network (SIPRNET) and passwords that allow access to the Federal Legal Information Through Electronics database.

(8) Identify any constraints (e.g., space limitations, time and funding).

b. Based on the notional JTF SJA template discussed in the section on forming the manning requirements above, a notional SJA equipment list is provided at Appendix A, "Notional Staff Judge Advocate Section Equipment and Capabilities."

7. Deployment

a. Deployment marks the beginning of the execution phase of the operation. Prior to a main body deployment, the JTF SJA researches and determines what legal authorities are in place and what legal authorities are necessary or desired to support the JTF mission. Authorities regarding the status, overflight, and ground transit of forces are usually most critical at this stage. The CJTF and higher headquarters must be alerted to any legal deficiencies as soon as possible to allow them to coordinate and address the deficiency. The JTF SJA or a representative should deploy with the advance party to provide guidance on HN support, contracting support, and contractor personnel integration; to liaise with law enforcement, judicial, and embassy authorities; to coordinate procedures for foreign claims, temporary refuge and asylum requests, arming and detention policies, and environmental law issues; and to resolve other legal issues identified in the mission analysis.

b. The JTF SJA ensures that all section personnel, including any augmentees, are trained and medically qualified to deploy. The JTF SJA establishes a deployment plan for the section that is integrated into the overall JTF plan. All personnel in the section should understand the deployment plan for section movement priorities. Because augmentees to the JTF may deploy from different staging areas, and arrive at different times and reception points, each member of the JTF SJA section must understand the reception, staging, onward movement, and integration plan and the joint personnel reception center process. In addition, the JTF SJA designates a closure element that ensures the section is present, accounted for, and operational. Finally, the JTF SJA is responsible for monitoring changes to the TPFDD and coordinating adjustments to the flow of SJA section personnel as necessary.

c. The JTF SJA ensures that all legal authorities are established with HNs to support the overflight and ground transit of forces. JTF SJA also will ensure that higher headquarters counterparts have addressed operational issues that could be impacted by international, multilateral and bilateral treaties, agreements and arrangements in all affected AORs. Reference the *DOD Electronic Foreign Clearance Guide* (https://www.fcg.pentagon.mil/fcg.cfm) for peacetime agreements and arrangements in place concerning overflight and personnel travel requirements. This document may be used as a starting position for understanding contingency response agreements with HNs.

8. Employment

a. Modern military operations take place in an increasingly complex geo-political environment. The classic scenario of defending against cross-border aggression represents only one of the challenges facing current JFCs. Stability operations, foreign humanitarian assistance operations, and civil-military operations present increased requirements for direct legal support to the JFC. In this ever-changing environment, the JTF SJA no longer functions primarily within the combat support and combat service support arenas. A member of the JFC's personal staff, the JTF SJA is an essential advisor on the myriad of legal issues associated with combat and noncombat operations.

b. Statesmanship and diplomacy are important factors. Such considerations and working with DOD and other US Government agencies, foreign government agencies, NGOs, and intergovernmental organizations may occupy a significant portion of the JFC's time. The JTF SJA assists the CJTF in working with these DOD and non-DOD organizations; for example, the International Committee of the Red Cross. At the same time, the JTF SJA ensures that the CJTF understands the laws, policies, treaties, and agreements that apply to US relations with the governments and inhabitants of foreign nations in the JTF's JOA and how those laws, policies, treaties, and agreements may affect current and future JTF operations.

c. The JTF SJA assists the CJTF in monitoring, assessing, planning, coordinating, directing, and controlling operations through direct participation on JTF boards, centers, cells, and working groups. For example, to support JTF current operations, the JTF SJA assigns judge advocates as watch officers to the various JTF operations centers. SJA watch officers are responsible for assisting their J-3 counterparts in the preparation of plans relating to current operations; assisting in the development of OPORDs and ROE and monitoring their execution with J-3 and/or J-5; preparing operational reports; providing inputs to requests for information; providing operational law advice; maintaining SJA section journals and files necessary to record operational activities; evaluating actions to identify operational deficiencies; developing methods to improve joint effectiveness; and keeping the SJA and counterparts at higher, lower, and adjacent headquarters appropriately informed utilizing the CIE. The JTF SJA also assigns judge advocates to support other critical boards and cells like the JTCB, where operational law expertise is absolutely essential to a proper analysis of whether planned strikes and time-sensitive and/or targets of opportunity comply with US obligations under the law of war; and the joint military police agency, where operational and international law expertise is similarly essential to ensure that the JTF's treatment of EPWs and detainees is in accordance with applicable law.

d. Information management is a critical challenge facing the JTF SJA in the CIE. The increased size of the area in which joint operations take place and the large number of command elements favors decentralized execution at the operational level. If information is key to understanding the operational environment, information overload caused by the massive volume of information transmitted by high-technology systems can significantly impede decision making.

e. The JTF SJA section must retain an operational focus. By staying ahead of tactical events, the section can anticipate potential operational challenges, and can develop timely, cogent, and proactive solutions. Allowing the JTF SJA section to remain too tactically focused could do a disservice to the JTF and to the component SJAs who look to the JTF SJA for operational guidance and intent.

9. Transition

The JTF SJA is responsible for transitioning legal support responsibilities to follow-on forces. Transition may occur between the JTF and another US command, a foreign command (e.g., HN or United Nations forces), or an organization under civilian control. Both organizations must prepare for and coordinate the transition to ensure an orderly transfer of authority and responsibility. The JTF SJA's responsibilities include the following:

a. Providing legal advice to the JFC and staff on conditions required to transfer command and other legal authority, including drafting necessary transition documents.

b. Assigning a representative to the transition cell.

c. Coordinating and approving procedures for transition of legal support tasks.

d. Reviewing and recommending a timeline and milestones for transition that optimizes legal conditions.

e. Monitoring the transition to ensure all legal requirements are accomplished.

10. Redeployment

a. Redeployment may begin at any point during JTF operations, so redeployment planning should begin as soon as possible. As with other phases in the JTF life cycle, redeployment may overlap the employment and transition phases. During redeployment, the JTF SJA sets section movement priorities; provides priorities and guidance for section recovery and reconstitution; and determines if deployment of additional personnel is required to assist with section redeployment activities.

b. As the JTF's mission ends, the JTF may require more legal support rather than less (e.g., to oversee "wrap-up" legal activities including contracts, claims settlement, property accountability, and any remaining good order and discipline issues). The JTF SJA must monitor the current situation in light of the JTF commander's intent and guidance and adjust the section's manning and individual responsibilities accordingly. The personnel and equipment identified for redeployment must be incorporated into the TPFDD process, and the security requirements of remaining section personnel must be coordinated with the appropriate JTF staff directorates or subordinate commander.

11. Lessons Learned

a. During execution, transition, and redeployment, the JTF SJA and legal section should capture and chronicle legal lessons learned. Use of lessons learned will ensure succeeding SJAs will have the benefit of the experiences of their predecessors.

b. Lessons learned should be captured in accordance with CCDR and Service requirements and submitted to both. Each CCDR and USJFCOM operates a lessons learned office responsible for the collection of lessons from the field, their distillation, and their introduction into the joint training process. Similarly, each service operates a lessons learned command dedicated to ensuring that the lessons of each operational unit are passed on in Service training to all forces. These Service lessons learned commands coordinate with USJFCOM to ensure that all lessons are available for integration into the joint training process.

c. Lessons learned should include, among other concerns, legal issues and access to resources including reach-back support to resolve them, equipment, billeting, personnel legal specialties, non-lawyer skill requirements, tour length appropriateness, and other operational matters that affect the provision of legal services.

d. The Center for Law and Military Operations is a joint, interagency, and multinational legal center responsible for: collecting and synthesizing data relating to legal issues arising in military operations; managing a central repository of information relating to such issues; and disseminating resources addressing these issues to facilitate the development of doctrine, organization, training, material, leadership, personnel, and facilities as these areas affect the military legal community.

APPENDIX A
NOTIONAL STAFF JUDGE ADVOCATE SECTION
EQUIPMENT AND CAPABILITIES

1. Notional Staff Judge Advocate Section Equipment

Figure A-1 represents a notional equipment list for SJA section personnel providing legal support to a land-based JTF. Most items will be obtained through JTF supply channels.

NOTIONAL STAFF JUDGE ADVOCATE SECTION EQUIPMENT LIST	
EQUIPMENT	**REQUIRED NUMBERS/ON HAND**
Basic Office Equipment:	
Deployable computer system **(Classified and Unclassified)** Including: Laptop Printer Copier Scanner Digital camera Extra batteries CAC reader(s) Electronic storage devices (e.g., CD, DVD) Data transfer devices (e.g., digital sender, facsimile) Digital recorders Accessories	
Storage Containers (Classified and Unclassified)	
Speech to Speech Translator System	
Phones, Secure Capable Phones and Cell Phones	
Mission-Specific Requirements	
Work/living space (hard stand, tent, etc)	
Radio Sets, field phones	
Truck/Utility Vehicles: e.g., Cargo/Troop Carrier/Command	
Generators (power generations section should determine requirement)	
Light Sets	

Figure A-1. Notional Staff Judge Advocate Section Equipment List

2. Notional Staff Judge Advocate Section Capabilities

Figure A-2 represents a notional capability list for SJA section personnel providing legal support to a land-based JTF.

NOTIONAL STAFF JUDGE ADVOCATE SECTION CAPABILITIES LIST	
CAPABILITY	**REQUIRED/ON HAND**
Security Clearances	
Electronic legal research capability	
Office Resources: CD FLITE Deployment CD Enduring Freedom/JAG Flag CD AF Publication Electronic Library CD US Code Service CD DLWills Electronic Judge Advocate Warfighting System (EJAWS) Resource Army Operational Law Handbook CD Joint Electronic Library CD Deployed Judge Advocate Resource Library (CLAMO) CD Military Justice Resources (Criminal Law Dept, The Judge Advocate General's School, USA) CD Rule of Law Handbook (CLAMO) CD Legal Assistance Management Resources (The Judge Advocate General's School, USA)	

Figure A-2. Notional Staff Judge Advocate Section Capabilities List

3. Web-Based Legal Resources

a. US Government and Department of Defense

(1) DOD Publications: http://www.dtic.mil/whs/directives/.

(2) US Code Service: http://uscode.house.gov/.

b. Air Force

(1) Air Force Judge Advocate General's Corps (WebFLITE): https://aflsa.jag.af.mil/cgi-bin/thome.cgi.

(2) WebFLITE - DOD Reference Materials: Operations and International Law: https://aflsa.jag.af.mil/GROUPS/ALL_FLITE/INTERNATIONAL/.

(3) WebFLITE Army resource materials: https://aflsa.jag.af.mil/GROUPS/ALL_FLITE/INTERNATIONAL/army.html.

(4) WebFLITE Navy and Marine Corps resource materials: https://aflsa.jag.af.mil/GROUPS/ALL_FLITE/INTERNATIONAL/sea.html.

(5) Air Force Publications: http://www.e-publishing.af.mil/.

c. **Army**

(1) US Army JAGC Net: https://www.jagcnet.army.mil/.

(2) Center for Law and Military Operations: https://www.jagcnet.army.mil/.

(3) Operational Law Handbook: https://www.jagcnet.army.mil/8525751D00557EFF/0/A86D78669E17E6F9852574DA005 E3ADF?opendocument.

(4) Army Publications: http://www.apd.army.mil/.

d. **Navy and Marines Corps**

(1) Navy JAG Manual: http://www.jag.navy.mil/library/instructions/JAGMAN2007.pdf.

(2) Commander's Handbook on the Law of Naval Operations: https://aflsa.jag.af.mil/GROUPS/ALL_FLITE/INTERNATIONAL/Navy/navsup.pdf.

(3) Manual for Courts-Martial: http://www.au.af.mil/au/awc/awcgate/law/mcm.pdf

(4) Marine Corps Publications: http://www.marines.mil/directiv.nsf/web+orders.

(5) Navy Directives: http://neds.daps.dla.mil/.

(6) WebFLITE Navy and Marine Corps resource materials: https://aflsa.jag.af.mil/GROUPS/ALL_FLITE/INTERNATIONAL/sea.html.

e. **Coast Guard**

(1) Coast Guard Legal Website: http://www.uscg.mil/legal/.

(2) Coast Guard Directives: http://www.uscg.mil/directives/cim.asp.

Intentionally Blank

APPENDIX B
REFERENCES

The development of JP 1-04 is based on the following primary references:

1. **General**

    a. *The National Security Act of 1947*, as amended (Title 50, USC, Section 401 et seq.).

    b. *Goldwater-Nichols DOD Reorganization Act of 1986* (Title 10, USC, Section 161 et seq.).

    c. *Manual for Courts-Martial, United States*.

    d. *Treaties Affairs*, http://www.state.gov/s/l/treaty/index.htm.

2. **Department of Defense**

    a. DOD Directive (DODD) 2311.01E, *DOD Law of War Program*.

    b. DODD 3025.15, *Military Assistance to Civil Authorities*.

    c. DODD 5100.3, *Support of the Headquarters of Combatant and Subordinate Joint Commands*.

    d. DODD 5145.01, *General Counsel of the Department of Defense*.

    e. DODD 5145.4, *Defense Legal Services Agency*.

    f. DODD 5530.3, *International Agreements*.

3. **Chairman of the Joint Chiefs of Staff**

    a. CJCSI 3100.01B, *Joint Strategic Planning System*.

    b. CJCSI 3121.01B, *Standing Rules of Engagement/Standing Rules for the Use of Force for US Forces*.

    c. CJCSI 3141.01D, *Management and Review of Campaign and Contingency Plans*.

    d. CJCSI 3150.25D, *Joint Lessons Learned Program*.

    e. CJCSI 5810.01D, *Implementation of the DOD Law of War Program*.

f. CJCSM 3122.03C, *Joint Operation Planning and Execution System Vol II: (Planning Formats)*.

g. CJCSM 3500.03B, *Joint Training Manual for the Armed Forces of the United States*.

h. CJCSM 3500.04E, *Universal Joint Task List*.

i. JP 1, *Doctrine for the Armed Forces of the United States*.

j. JP 1-02, *Department of Defense Dictionary of Military and Associated Terms*.

k. JP 3-0, *Joint Operations*.

l. JP 3-08, *Interorganizational Coordination During Joint Operations*.

m. JP 3-13, *Information Operations*.

n. JP 3-16, *Multinational Operations*.

o. JP 3-30, *Command and Control for Joint Air Operations*.

p. JP 3-33, *Joint Task Force Headquarters*.

q. JP 3-60, *Joint Targeting*.

r. JP 5-0, *Joint Operation Planning*.

4. **Military Department Publications**

a. DA Pam 27-1, *Treaties Governing Land Warfare*.

b. Army Regulation 27-1, *Legal Services, Judge Advocate Legal Services*.

c. Field Manual 1-04, *Legal Operations to the Operational Army*.

d. Operational Law Handbook (JA 422), Center for Law and Military Operations, The 39 Judge Advocate General's School, United States Army.

e. NWP 1-14M, The *Commander's Handbook on the Law of Naval Operations*.

f. Air Force Operations and the Law, *A Guide for Air, Space and Cyber Forces*, Air Force Judge Advocate General's Department.

g. Commandant, US Coast Guard Instruction (COMDTINST) M16247.1A, *Maritime Law Enforcement Manual*.

h. COMDTINST M1000.6 (series), *Coast Guard Personnel Manual.*

Intentionally Blank

APPENDIX C
ADMINISTRATIVE INSTRUCTIONS

1. User Comments

Users in the field are highly encouraged to submit comments on this publication to: Commander, United States Joint Forces Command, Joint Warfighting Center, ATTN: Doctrine and Education Group, 116 Lake View Parkway, Suffolk, VA 23435-2697. These comments should address content (accuracy, usefulness, consistency, and organization), writing, and appearance.

2. Authorship

The lead agent for this publication is the US Joint Forces Command. The Joint Staff doctrine sponsor for this publication is the Legal Counsel for the Chairman of the Joint Chiefs of Staff.

3. Supersession

This publication supersedes JP 1-04, 01 March 2007, *Legal Support to Military Operations*.

4. Change Recommendations

a. Recommendations for urgent changes to this publication should be submitted electronically to the Lead Agent, with information copies sent to the Joint Staff J-7 Joint Doctrine and Education Division and to the US Joint Forces Command Joint Warfighting Center, Doctrine and Education Group.

b. Routine changes should be submitted electronically to the US Joint Forces Command Joint Warfighting Center, Doctrine and Education Group, and info the Lead Agent and the Joint Staff J-7 Joint Doctrine and Education Division.

c. When a Joint Staff directorate submits a proposal to the Chairman of the Joint Chiefs of Staff that would change source document information reflected in this publication, that directorate will include a proposed change to this publication as an enclosure to its proposal. The military Services and other organizations are requested to notify the Joint Staff J-7 when changes to source documents reflected in this publication are initiated.

d. Record of Changes:

CHANGE NUMBER	COPY NUMBER	DATE OF CHANGE	DATE ENTERED	POSTED BY	REMARKS

5. Distribution of Publications

Local reproduction is authorized and access to unclassified publications is unrestricted. However, access to and reproduction authorization for classified joint publications must be in accordance with DOD 5200.1-R, *Information Security Program.*

6. Distribution of Electronic Publications

a. Joint Staff J-7 will not print copies of JPs for distribution. Electronic versions are available on JDEIS at https://jdeis.js.mil (NIPRNET), and https://jdeis.js.smil.mil (SIPRNET) and on the JEL at http://www.dtic.mil/doctrine (NIPRNET).

b. Only approved joint publications and joint test publications are releasable outside the combatant commands, Services, and Joint Staff. Release of any classified joint publication to foreign governments or foreign nationals must be requested through the local embassy (Defense Attaché Office) to DIA Foreign Liaison Office, PO-FL, Room 1E811, 7400 Pentagon, Washington, DC 20301-7400.

c. CD-ROM. Upon request of a JDDC member, the Joint Staff J-7 will produce and deliver one CD-ROM with current joint publications.

GLOSSARY
PART I — ABBREVIATIONS AND ACRONYMS

AOR	area of responsibility
APEX	Adaptive Planning and Execution
CAP	crisis action planning
CCDR	combatant commander
CIE	collaborative information environment
CJCS	Chairman of the Joint Chiefs of Staff
CJCSI	Chairman of the Joint Chiefs of Staff instruction
CJCSM	Chairman of the Joint Chiefs of Staff manual
CJTF	commander, joint task force
COA	course of action
COMDTINST	Commandant, United States Coast Guard instruction
DA	Department of the Army
DAF	Department of the Air Force
DIA	Defense Intelligence Agency
DOD	Department of Defense
DODD	Department of Defense directive
DON	Department of the Navy
DTRA	Defense Threat Reduction Agency
EPW	enemy prisoner of war
GC	general counsel
HN	host nation
HQ	headquarters
J-1	manpower and personnel directorate of a joint staff
J-3	operations directorate of a joint staff
J-5	plans directorate of a joint staff
JA	judge advocate
JAG	judge advocate general
JCS	Joint Chiefs of Staff
JFC	joint force commander
JLSE	joint legal support element
JMD	joint manning document
JOA	joint operations area
JOC	joint operations center
JP	joint publication
JPG	joint planning group
JSPS	Joint Strategic Planning System
JTCB	joint targeting coordination board

JTF	joint task force
JTP	joint training plan
LC	legal counsel
LOAC	law of armed conflict
MEDEVAC	medical evacuation
NGB	National Guard Bureau
NGO	nongovernmental organization
NSCS	National Security Council System
NWP	Navy warfare publication
OPORD	operation order
PPBE	Planning, Programming, Budgeting, and Execution
RC	Reserve Component
ROE	rules of engagement
RUF	rules for the use of force
SECAF	Secretary of the Air Force
SecDef	Secretary of Defense
SIPRNET	SECRET Internet Protocol Router Network
SJA	staff judge advocate
SJFHQ	standing joint force headquarters
SOF	special operations forces
TJAG	the judge advocate general
TPFDD	time-phased force and deployment data
USC	United States Code
USSOCOM	United States Special Operations Command
USSTRATCOM	United States Strategic Command
USTRANSCOM	United States Transportation Command

archipelagic sea lanes passage. None. (Approved for removal from JP 1-02.)

Chairman's program assessment. None. (Approved for removal from JP 1-02.)

Chairman's program recommendations. None. (Approved for removal from JP 1-02.)

collective self-defense. None. (Approved for removal from JP 1-02.)

individual self-defense. None. (Approved for removal from JP 1-02.)

integrated priority list. A list of a combatant commander's highest priority requirements, prioritized across Service and functional lines, defining shortfalls in key programs that, in the judgment of the combatant commander, adversely affect the capability of the combatant commander's forces to accomplish their assigned mission. Also called **IPL.** (Approved for incorporation into JP 1-02.)

judge advocate. An officer of the Judge Advocate General's Corps of the Army, Air Force, Marine Corps, Navy, and the United States Coast Guard who is designated as a judge advocate. Also called **JA.** (Approved for incorporation into JP 1-02.)

law of armed conflict. See **law of war.** (Approved for incorporation into JP 1-02 with JP 1-04 as the source JP.)

law of war. That part of international law that regulates the conduct of armed hostilities. Also called **the law of armed conflict.** (Approved for incorporation into JP 1-02 with JP 1-04 as the source JP.)

military necessity. None. (Approved for removal from JP 1-02.)

protected persons/places. Persons (such as enemy prisoners of war) and places (such as hospitals) that enjoy special protections under the law of war. They may or may not be marked with protected emblems. (Approved for incorporation into JP 1-02 with JP 1-04 as the source JP.)

rules of engagement. Directives issued by competent military authority that delineate the circumstances and limitations under which United States forces will initiate and/or continue combat engagement with other forces encountered. Also called **ROE.** (JP 1-02. SOURCE: JP 1-04)

self-defense. None. (Approved for removal from JP 1-02.)

staff judge advocate. A judge advocate so designated in the Army, Air Force, or Marine Corps, and the principal legal advisor of a Navy, Coast Guard, or joint force command who is a judge advocate. Also called **SJA.** (JP 1-02. SOURCE: JP 1-04)

transit passage. None. (Approved for removal from JP 1-02.)

JOINT DOCTRINE PUBLICATIONS HIERARCHY

JP 1 JOINT DOCTRINE

JP 1-0 PERSONNEL	JP 2-0 INTELLIGENCE	JP 3-0 OPERATIONS	JP 4-0 LOGISTICS	JP 5-0 PLANS	JP 6-0 COMMUNICATIONS SYSTEM

All joint publications are organized into a comprehensive hierarchy as shown in the chart above. **Joint Publication (JP) 1-04** is in the **Personnel** series of joint doctrine publications. The diagram below illustrates an overview of the development process:

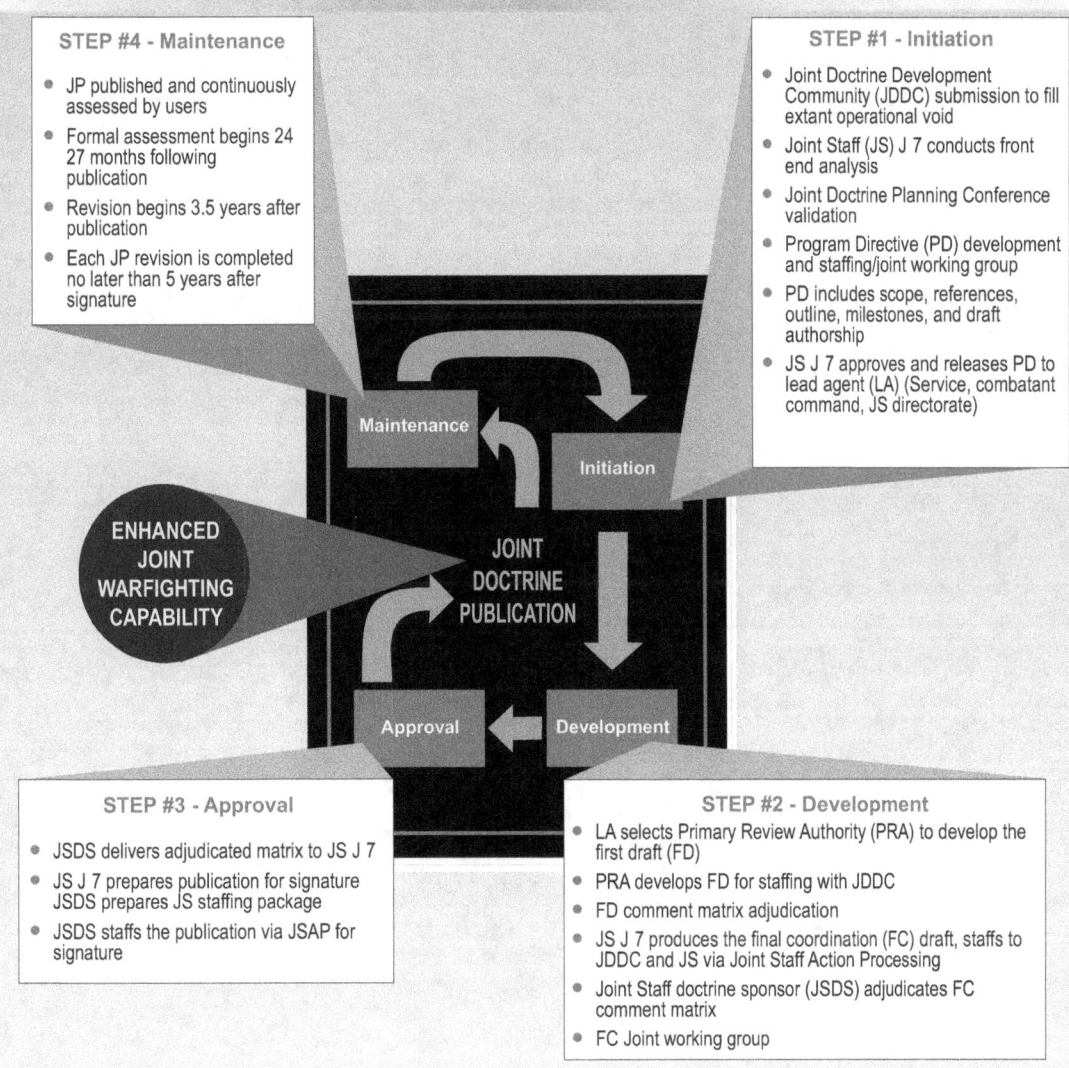

STEP #4 - Maintenance

- JP published and continuously assessed by users
- Formal assessment begins 24 27 months following publication
- Revision begins 3.5 years after publication
- Each JP revision is completed no later than 5 years after signature

STEP #1 - Initiation

- Joint Doctrine Development Community (JDDC) submission to fill extant operational void
- Joint Staff (JS) J 7 conducts front end analysis
- Joint Doctrine Planning Conference validation
- Program Directive (PD) development and staffing/joint working group
- PD includes scope, references, outline, milestones, and draft authorship
- JS J 7 approves and releases PD to lead agent (LA) (Service, combatant command, JS directorate)

ENHANCED JOINT WARFIGHTING CAPABILITY

Maintenance

Initiation

JOINT DOCTRINE PUBLICATION

Approval

Development

STEP #3 - Approval

- JSDS delivers adjudicated matrix to JS J 7
- JS J 7 prepares publication for signature JSDS prepares JS staffing package
- JSDS staffs the publication via JSAP for signature

STEP #2 - Development

- LA selects Primary Review Authority (PRA) to develop the first draft (FD)
- PRA develops FD for staffing with JDDC
- FD comment matrix adjudication
- JS J 7 produces the final coordination (FC) draft, staffs to JDDC and JS via Joint Staff Action Processing
- Joint Staff doctrine sponsor (JSDS) adjudicates FC comment matrix
- FC Joint working group